The Story of
THE COMMON MARKET

The Story of
THE COMMON MARKET

by Katharine Savage

Illustrated with photographs and maps

New York   *Henry Z. Walck, Inc.*

382   Savage, Katharine
  S   The story of the Common Market.
          Walck, 1970
              192p. photos. maps

              Bibliography: p.185-186. Index
              Readable account of the formation,
          development, and workings of the
          European Economic Community.

              1. European Economic Community
              2. Europe -   Economic policy
              I. Title

This Main Entry catalog card may be reproduced without permission.

I dedicate this book
to Kathy—my eldest grandchild

ACKNOWLEDGMENTS

I would like to thank the many friends and colleagues who have helped me in the preparation of this book. I especially wish to express my gratitude to Mr. Derek Prag, Director of the European Community Information Service in London, who read the manuscript and from his wide experience of the subject gave me invaluable guidance. I am also very grateful to Mr. Franco Ciarnelli, Director of the European Community Information Service in New York, and Mr. Leonard B. Tennyson, Director of the European Community Information Service in Washington, and their staffs, for their help and good advice. It is only fair to them all to state that the final conclusions are my own.

Once more I must record my great gratitude to Gillian Winger who has now worked with me on five books, and on whose support and skill I depend increasingly with each publication.

My thanks are due to Richard Natkeil, F.R.G.S., who drew the maps, and to the following organizations for permission to reproduce copyright photographs:

European Community Information Service: pp. 10, 71, 76, 78, 83, 91, 95, 98, 101, 107, 110, 123, 125, 127, 155, 164, 169, 179; Council of Europe: p. 56; Realités: p. 37; Camera Press Ltd: pp. 133, 145, 147; United Nations: p. 28; Wide World Photos: pp. 44, 53.

Katharine Savage

CONTENTS

Headquarters of the Commission of the European Communities in Brussels

1

THE SIX GET TOGETHER

The European Economic Community, better known throughout the world today by the simpler title of the Common Market, is a living expression of the desperate need of the countries of Western Europe for prosperity and peace.

In the midst of the widespread devastation and appalling poverty which followed the Second World War, a few outstanding statesmen examined the idea of a European Community and worked on it until they produced a long-term plan to bring their countries into a working partnership for the common good. They saw in European unity a means of eliminating the cutthroat competition in armaments and power politics that leads nations into war, and they approached their task with great urgency, for it was evident that a third world war could end only in total disaster and the destruction of civilization.

The principles and provisions of the European Economic Community, the EEC, were established by the Treaty of Rome, signed on the Capitoline Hill in the heart of the ancient capital on March 25, 1957. In the course of preliminary conferences, long discussions and delicate negotiations, representatives of Belgium, the Federal Republic of Germany, France, Italy, Luxembourg and the Netherlands had hammered out the broad outlines of agreement on a policy of gradual economic and eventual political union. When the Foreign Ministers of the six countries finally gathered in Rome to sign the Treaty, they solemnly pledged their governments to respect the terms and carry out the obligations contained in the historic document.

The Treaty in its present form acts as a joint constitution governing the economic affairs of the Six, regulating their relations with one another and their dealings with the outside world. In the same way that the constitutions of individual countries can be amended to meet changing circumstances or particular needs, the Treaty of Rome allows its members the right to review and revise the laws by mutual consent. It views the lowering of customs barriers and eventual free trade among the Six as a way to ensure a fair share in steadily increasing prosperity for all the member peoples. But above all, the Treaty of Rome regards economic union as a first step in the direction of "an ever closer union among the European peoples."

There is a provision in the Treaty giving the Six the right to admit any other European state willing to accept the established conditions of membership. But each of the Six has an equal right to block a new entry by imposing a veto on its application, and in actual fact by the Spring of 1970, owing to a combination of events which the most forward-looking planners could not possibly have foreseen, no other nation had been permitted to join the Six.

The opening passages of the Treaty, which are officially called the Preamble, summarize the basic principles and ultimate aims of European unity. The Treaty then proceeds Article by Article, and there are two hundred and forty-eight Articles in all, to build the framework of progressive partnership and gradual integration. The architects of the Treaty framed the terms carefully because they were looking ahead to a time when nations would give up their national sovereignty, and they saw that in preparing for such an important happening they must move with great caution. They regarded financial agreement as the essential first step on the road to political union, and they tried to devise a system whereby the Common Market nations would pool their industrial and agricultural resources, and their knowledge and skills, for the benefit of all.

As a final objective, supporters of the European Economic Community envisaged an era of European accord and prosperity when nationalism would lose its meaning and people would voluntarily accept the legislation of a supranational European Parliament. Instead of being French, German, Italian or Dutch, they would be proud simply to be European.

The political leaders who steered their governments toward the formation of the EEC came from a variety of European countries. Foremost among them was Robert Schuman, the French Foreign Minister who had been the driving force behind the European Coal and Steel Community—an organization formed in 1953 for joint industrial cooperation—which proved to be the forerunner of the Common Market. Important also were Konrad Adenauer, the first Chancellor of the Federal Republic of Germany, the "grand old man" of German politics; and Alcide de Gasperi, who had been prominent in the Italian Resistance Movement during the Second World War and, as leader of the Italian Christian Democratic Party, was Prime Minister of eight successive postwar governments. These three champions of European unity were highly respected in their own countries, and their words carried weight in international politics. Though they were of different nationalities, there were important similarities in their backgrounds. All three were brought up as devout Catholics and retained their faith in later life. They viewed the Common Market not only in the light of an economic and political merger, but also as an opportunity to build a Christian bastion in Europe against a decline in moral standards and the dangers of disbelief. It is interesting that each of the three grew up with German as his mother tongue. Schuman, the Frenchman, was born in Luxembourg and brought up in the province of Lorraine, then under German rule. Adenauer, the German, spent his boyhood in the Rhineland city of Cologne; and de Gasperi, the Italian, was born in the mountainous region of the Tyrol which then belonged to Austria.

There were many other active planners of a united Europe; foremost among them were Jean Monnet, a Frenchman who won the nickname Monsieur Europe because of his unbounded faith in the fine future of the United States of Europe; and Paul-Henri Spaak, who led the Belgian Government in London during the German occupation of his country and returned to high office after the Allied victory. In a completely different way, Charles de Gaulle, leader of the Free French Government during the last war, ex-President of the Fifth Republic and a fanatical advocate of the glory of France, pictured a united Europe. All these men and many others who worked for European unity had lived through the horrors of two wars. They were shocked by the waste and suffering and longed for the promise of permanent peace.

The Common Market was the goal of many ardent "Europeans," but they did not achieve it without a struggle. It was a dream which seemed at times too remote to bring down to earth and too complicated to come true. Even the men who shared the same vision had very differ-

European Economic Community Countries

ent methods of approach. It took time, knowledge, patience and resolution to smooth out the humps and remove the hurdles on the road to agreement. The story of the Common Market is made up of politics and personalities, ideas and ideals, hard bargaining and high principles. It has come into being through modern human endeavor loosely linked to historical precedent, for the territory of the Six covers almost the same area in Europe as the first Christian empire founded by the great warrior Charlemagne over a thousand years ago.

The European Economic Community is a positive reaction to years of strife and bloodshed; and the Treaty of Rome is a blueprint for European unity. It was drawn up by painstaking, peace-loving men as a defense against nuclear warfare and the breakdown of everything that most Europeans value and respect. They pictured Europe so united in purpose that war between the nations would be unthinkable, and strong enough to deter outside agression. If the plan succeeds, in the course of time, the organization of the United States of Europe could resemble the political setup of the United States of America, where over 200,000,000 people live in a federation without frontiers.

But there are obstacles in the way of the United States of Europe which were not present when European pioneers formed the United States of America. Foremost among them are the existing individual political systems, the independent languages, the traditional cultures and the established national identities of the European countries.

In 1780 representatives of twelve colonies drew up the Constitution of the United States of America, proclaiming that every citizen should enjoy equal opportunity irrespective of race, or creed, but it was a foregone conclusion that in order to take an active part in the life of the nation they should all speak English. Germans and Italians, Poles and Swedes, Hungarians and Czechs arrived speaking entirely different languages and dialects, but their children went to school and learned the language of the country. In the same way, these European immigrants imported their own cultures, and the next generation grafted them onto American roots so that they grew up in a fresh climate with a New World look.

The United States has a Federal capital and a single Constitution, a common currency and free trade throughout the nation, a supreme court and state schools, and a national system of defense. But whereas Americans tamed a wilderness to build a modern nation, Europeans find themselves in a very different situation. It is bound to take time to convince the citizens of separate countries of the wisdom of surrendering established institutions and treasured independence, for the promise of peace through federal union.

This book is a survey of current European problems and an attempt to present them in their true perspective against the somber background of two world wars. It is a brief history of a new development in European thinking, and a daring experiment in international cooperation. It is also a tribute to the men who had the vision and the conviction to set it in motion.

2

A DIVIDED EUROPE

LOOKING BACK over the history of Western Europe during the last century, it appears that until the 1950's there was never a period when France and Germany were in a position to negotiate with each other on equal terms. The provisions of the peace treaties which concluded the wars of 1870 and 1914 were so hard on the defeated nations—first France and then Germany—that they bred a sense of injustice and fostered hatred and distrust. National leaders inflamed the resentment of the people into an ardent patriotism and a desire for revenge that ended tragically in war.

Franco-German hostility came to a head in 1870. At this time William I was King of Prussia, but the actual power lay in the hands of Otto von Bismarck, who, through the severity of his rule, earned the name of the Iron Chancellor. Bismarck was determined to unite the many German principalities into a single mighty empire under Prussian leadership. But he had to move very carefully, for he was afraid that France would oppose his ambitions and turn the German princes against him. He built up a highly efficient military force and waited. When a dispute arose between the French and German governments over the succession to the Spanish throne, Bismarck tricked the French into thinking that they had been insulted and humiliated. They clamored for reprisal and rashly declared war on Prussia; whereupon the German states gave Prussia their support.

This was the opportunity that Bismarck had been hoping for. He sent in an army and routed the French forces by superior tactics and arms. In four weeks the Prussians encircled Paris. The French put up a gallant defense, but they were ill-prepared. After four months' siege, the people ran out of food and the army had no ammunition. The guns were silent on the ramparts and the inhabitants were reduced to eating rats. On a bitter December night, the snow-covered city surrendered and the Germans marched in.

On January 18, 1871 the Prussian king, William I, was crowned the first emperor of a united Germany. The ceremony took place in the resplendent Hall of Mirrors in the Palace of Versailles, the scene of former French grandeur. The Germans followed up their victory with a triumphal procession through the streets of Paris, while the Parisians remained indoors behind closed shutters.

French shame and bitterness at defeat was intensified when, by the Treaty of Frankfurt, the Prussian victors laid claim to the long-disputed provinces of Alsace and Lorraine, with the beautiful city of Strasbourg. They also took the mighty fortress of Metz, a key point in French military defense.

Just over forty years later, when French anger was still smoldering, Europe was once more aflame with war. Trouble first flared up in the Balkans—traditionally, a hotbed of discontent—where the heir to the Austrian throne was assassinated by a fanatical member of a nationalist group opposed to Austrian rule. The German emperor, William II, encouraged Austria to fight, to avenge the crime, and used the Balkan disturbance as an excuse for a European war. He then attacked in the west, hoping to gain complete supremacy in Western Europe.

The German High Command was fully prepared for the war, with highly trained armies and an immense stock of weapons. On August 2, 1914, German forces crossed the Belgian frontier and pressed on into France, ignoring a pact which guaranteed Belgian neutrality. At this time most European nations were bound up in a complicated system of pacts and alliances. Britain and Russia immediately honored their pact with France and declared war on Germany. The conflict rapidly widened into the First World War, with the armed forces of Great Britain and the Commonwealth, Belgium, France, Italy, Japan, Russia and Serbia (now part of Yugoslavia) ranged against the Austro-Hungarian Empire, Bulgaria, Germany and Turkey. In 1917 the Russian armies stopped fighting as a result of the internal unrest which ended in the Bolshevik Revolution. In the same year the strength of the Western Allies was greatly strengthened when the United States declared war against Germany, and dispatched fresh troops to reinforce the exhausted armies on the Western front.

In November 1918, Germany finally capitulated; but during the four years of war—on the blood-soaked battlefields of France, Belgium, Northern Italy, Poland, Russia, the Balkans, the Middle East, and on the high seas—millions of men had died and millions more had been terribly injured. When an armistice was declared, the war-weary troops of many nations laid down their arms with thankfulness and relief.

Of all the warring nations, France had suffered most. For the duration of the war the fiercest battles were fought on French territory. In the region between Paris and the Belgian frontier, the front line swayed backwards and forwards over a changing no-man's-land until the country was churned up into a cratered blackened waste, and the towns and villages were flattened into piles of rubble.

Worse still, nearly a fifth of all the fighting men of France were killed. Hardly a family survived the war

Treaty of Versailles

intact and these losses had a profound effect on French
policy in the following years. In the 1930's—when Adolf
Hitler came to power in Germany and bold decisions were
needed in neighboring countries—so many of the young
Frenchmen who would have taken a leading part in public affairs were dead, that the government was largely
in the hands of elderly politicians who were immensely
patriotic, but tired and very cautious.

When the representatives of the victorious Allied
nations assembled to frame a peace treaty, their main
concern was to ensure that Germany would never be in
a position to attack again. They tried to combine punish-
ment with justice. Every country demanded some particular reward, but they all agreed that German aggression
must be crushed once and for all. Finally, the Allied leaders drew up the Treaty of Versailles and summoned a
German delegation to the famous Hall of Mirrors to study
the text. The terms were extremely severe, but the Germans were in no position to refuse. They signed the treaty
by which they agreed to disband the Army, scrap the
Navy, and committed the German Government to pay
large reparations in money and goods to compensate for
war damage. In addition, France took back Alsace and
Lorraine, and other strips of territory were pared off the
German frontiers and handed over to neighboring nations. Moreover, all the German colonies in Africa were
proclaimed trust territories and placed under interna-

tional control. The Emperor William II, accompanied by his son the Crown Prince—frequently caricatured in the British press as "little Willie"—had already fled to Holland, and Germany was declared a republic.

The German people were stunned, for the surrender came as a shattering blow. They had realized through the shortages at home and the casualties on the Western front that the situation was serious; but they had such faith in their hitherto invincible armies that they never really faced up to the possibility of defeat. Suddenly they found themselves humbled before the world and compelled to admit that Germany was no longer a great power.

Humiliation was followed by real hardship. The German mark, which before the war had been worth twenty-five cents, was so drastically devalued that for most workingmen a week's wages could scarcely buy a loaf of bread, and they needed millions of marks to pay the rent or buy a suit. Prudent families who had economized in order to provide for the future lost their life's savings.

But the Germans are an industrious people. They got down to work and for a time it looked as if they might win through. Unfortunately for world peace, a financial depression started in the United States in the late 1920's and spread to Europe. In Germany the frail economy collapsed under the strain. Factories closed down and all over the country men and women were thrown out of work. They had no money to fall back on so they were

utterly destitute. By 1933 six-million Germans were un-
employed, and many of them were starving.

At this time of national despair the compelling voice
of Adolf Hitler made its first real impact, stirring the
people to rebellion and revenge. Hitler was Austrian, an
impoverished political agitator, with a record of personal
failure and a grudge against life. As a young man he lived
in a home for tramps in Vienna, doing odd jobs and paint-
ing poor pictures. In the First World War he served in
the German Army, and rose to the rank of corporal. After
the armistice he returned to civilian life and devoted his
whole being to politics.

Hitler had two ambitions: personal leadership and
German supremacy. He set out to achieve them by any
means, fair or foul. He climbed to power on lies and empty
promises, through the misery of the German people. They
were out of work and he promised them jobs; they were
hungry and he tempted them with the prospect of plenty.
They were downcast and he told them that they were a
master race destined to conquer the surrounding nations.
At the same time he gave them an outlet for their pent-up
anger by accusing the Jewish people of causing German
defeat and every other misfortune. He urged the Germans
to persecute the Jews and wipe them out. Hitler's followers
called themselves National Socialists, Nazis for short, and
chose the crooked cross, or swastika, as their emblem.

To begin with, most Germans regarded Hitler with

scorn or distaste. But he won them over by high-powered oratory and subtle propaganda, and above all, by providing them with work and wages.

In 1933 there was an acute political crisis, and Hitler seized his opportunity. By devious means, and for the lack of rival leadership, he took over the German Government. From that moment he acted as a supreme dictator and ruled without conscience or pity. He recruited a large force of Gestapo, or secret police, as a special instrument of cruelty in a reign of terror.

Hitler did not hesitate to sweep aside the restrictions of the Versailles Treaty, and very soon factories all over Germany secretly began to produce tanks and guns, aircraft and submarines. His own bodyguard of brown-coated, jack-booted storm troopers grew into an army.

The rest of the world watched the rise of Hitler, at first with amazement and then with dismay. But he had won a measure of toleration in the West by condemning communism as a world menace, for most leaders in Europe and the United States distrusted and feared the Bolshevik regime. In fact Hitler had announced his political program in a vast volume called *Mein Kampf* (My Struggle). But his beliefs and intentions were so barbaric that few people took them seriously. One notable exception was Winston Churchill who, as a member of the British Parliament, repeatedly warned the world against the dangers of Nazism.

At the time of the signing of the Versailles Treaty, Woodrow Wilson, President of the United States, had presented to the assembled company a new plan for world peace. He proposed a League of Nations, an international organization, where states could settle their disputes by peaceful discussion instead of by armed force. The League gave new hope to many harassed statesmen who were seeking a just settlement for the future, and they readily accepted President Wilson's plan.

The League of Nations came into being in 1920 and played an active, though diminishing, role in world affairs until the outbreak of the Second World War. The League failed in its major purpose, mainly for lack of American support. For, though President Wilson had inspired the other nations to form the League, the United States Government refused to join it. At the end of the war the American people had turned away from Europe and adopted a policy of "isolationism." It was an understandable attitude, for many of them had gone to the New World to escape from violence, persecution and political entanglement, and to build a new life. They had been drawn back into one European war and they feared that an international organization like the League of Nations would involve them in another.

In Europe also the nations drifted apart. If they had stood firmly together they might have blocked Hitler's triumphal progress. But France was weakened by her

Palais des Nations, the former headquarters of the League of Nations in Geneva

losses in the First World War; while Britain was committed to a policy of disarmament and was ruled by men who simply could not grasp the Hitler menace. They had set their hearts on peace and they found it impossible to believe that the despised Austrian upstart was really capable of plunging the world into war.

Hitler was the only leader who knew where he was going. He took advantage of the weakness of the Western nations and gambled on their evident desire for peace. His first open gesture of defiance was to move troops into the demilitarized zone of the Rhineland, bordering France. His next move was to take over Austria in 1938. The following year, despite a solemn undertaking to respect Czech independence, he occupied Czechoslovakia. Both countries were riddled with Nazi agents, the people were powerless to resist and Hitler conquered them without firing a shot.

At last, after the Czechoslovakian betrayal, Western leaders saw Hitler in his true colors. They began to rearm, but it was far too late.

In August 1939, in order to secure his eastern frontier from attack, Hitler signed a nonaggression pact with Joseph Stalin, a fellow dictator all powerful in the Soviet Union, whom he had always branded as his archenemy. A few weeks later Hitler launched a massive attack on Poland, trusting that France and Britain would be too hesitant to fulfill their pledge to defend Polish independence. However, he was soon proved wrong, for by September 3, 1939 Britain and France had declared war on Nazi Germany, and the world was confronted by the gruesome reality of total war.

3

A WORLD AFLAME WITH WAR

FOR THE SECOND TIME in just over twenty years Belgium, Britain and France stood face to face with enemy aggression. The noble design for world peace had broken down, and the carefully laid plans for restricting German might had not worked. German armies were on the warpath once more, and the sons of the men who had fought in the First World War were being called up to settle the sequel.

When France and Britain fulfilled their pledge to Poland, and declared war on Nazi Germany, there were no patriotic demonstrations and no enthusiasm in either country. The general attitude had changed since 1914 when French soldiers marched to war amid cheering crowds, with their regimental colors flying and their bands playing, and British audiences thunderously applauded stage stars who appeared against a background of Union Jacks singing:

> We don't want to lose you
> But, we think you ought to go;
> 'Cause your King and your Country
> Both need you so.

By the time Hitler came to power, war was no longer glorified. Most people regarded it as a colossal political failure and blamed the men at the top. Once the British were aroused they fought magnificently, but the "theirs but to do and die" sentiments of the nineteenth century had disappeared forever.

In the old days, men went off to war to protect their families from the enemy; but it was obvious when Nazi forces stormed into Poland with columns of tanks and wave after wave of dive bombers that there was no escape for the civilian population. They were unarmed but in the front line just the same.

The Poles fought with tremendous courage, until they were totally overcome by the armed massacre of Hitler's lightning war. Parachutists landed behind the Polish lines and cut communications, dive bombers roared down on military targets and also wrecked Polish towns and cities; and the tanks closed in, forming a relentless wall of steel. Stalin took advantage of his pact with Hitler and marched in to snatch a slice of Eastern Poland. In four weeks Polish resistance ended, and the people were left helpless under Nazi oppression.

During the following winter the Russians defeated Finland after a two-month war, and in the spring of 1940 Hitler occupied Denmark and conquered Norway. Units of the British Army and Navy had fought with the Norwegians, and the British people were indignant at the defeat. In a rising storm of protest Neville Chamberlain, who had been Prime Minister during the difficult years preceding the war, was forced to resign and Winston Churchill accepted the invitation of King George VI to form an all-party government to lead the country.

On May 10, within a few hours of Churchill's appointment, Hitler launched the long-awaited attack on the Western front. The opening assault hit Holland where the Dutch had counted on an elaborate system of water defenses to protect them against invasion. But German armor swept in before the frontier guards had time to open the sluice gates, and in five days Holland was beaten and the Dutch royal family had escaped to England.

The Belgian, French and British Armies braced themselves for the coming battle. At this time of acute peril, the French Chief of Staff, General Gamelin, held the Allied High Command. Unfortunately, he, like other leading French commanders, had gained his military experience during the First World War, and his ideas were out of date. Because he had not grasped the techniques of modern warfare, and had no conception of the mobility and power of Hitler's armies and air force, he based his tactics on prepared forts and established armored positions.

At the outbreak of the Second World War the French veteran commander, Marshal Pétain, was eighty-five years old. He had retired from active service before the First World War, but early in 1916, at the age of sixty-two, he was recalled to take over the important defense of Verdun, against a gigantic German attack. He inspired his men by his own fearlessness and they adored him. When, in the face of almost overwhelming enemy pressure, Pétain issued the famous Order of the Day: "They shall not pass," despite fearful casualties in the French ranks, they never did. In 1940 Pétain was a national hero and extremely influential in French military planning. He had favored the construction of the Maginot Line, a series of forts along the Franco-German frontier, linked by an elaborate system of underground communications, and he considered it impregnable.

Everyone expected the spearhead of German attack by the traditional route through Belgium. But the German High Command had other plans. While some armored columns advanced into Belgium against stiff resistance, the main attack struck north of the Maginot Line in the hilly region of the Ardennes. Pétain had decided that owing to the steep and rugged terrain this section was not dangerous. The German High Command knew through their spies that it was thinly manned by second-class units and horse cavalry, and they also knew that the Ardennes hills were no obstacle to modern tanks and equipment. The inexperienced troops did not stand a chance against the German onslaught. They were paralyzed by dive bombing and scattered by massive armored divisions. The Germans breached the front after four days of fighting, outflanked the Maginot Line and fanned out through France. It took the leading tanks only eight days to reach the English Channel at Abbeville, just south of Boulogne, and to cut the Allied Armies in two. By what seemed almost a miracle, 338,000 men of the British and French forces were rescued from the beleaguered beaches of Dunkirk, near the Franco-Belgian frontier. But Winston Churchill warned the nation that wars were not won by evacuations, and the situation in France grew rapidly worse.

Since 1922 Italy had been ruled by Benito Mussolini, head of a political party known as the Fascists. Fascism, like Nazism, was a totalitarian one-party regime, and Hitler and Mussolini had much in common. They had publicly proclaimed their mutual aims by signing a treaty of friendship which they termed "The Pact of Steel."

On June 12, Mussolini, hoping for a share in the fruits of an easy victory, joined forces with his fellow dictator. He declared war on Britain and France, and sent an army into Southern France. On the same day, Paris was declared an open city, which meant that the French would not defend it against German attack. The government moved first to Tours and then further south to Bordeaux.

In a desperate attempt to stem the tide of defeat, the staunch patriot Paul Reynaud was appointed Prime Minister; Marshal Pétain, Deputy Prime Minister; and General Gamelin was replaced by the seventy-four-year-old General Weygand. In the new government Colonel Charles de Gaulle, a comparatively unknown officer in an infantry regiment, was chosen to be Under Secretary of War. In these dangerous days the leadership of France was violently divided between men like Paul Reynaud and Charles de Gaulle, who were determined not to treat with the Germans and to continue the war at all cost, possibly from North Africa; and the defeatists led by Marshal Pétain, General Weygand and a career politician named Pierre Laval, who saw no future in further resistance.

By mid-June, when the French Armies were in full retreat everywhere, de Gaulle displayed his outstanding talent for leadership for the first time. He flew to London in a Royal Air Force plane to try to organize the evacuation of the loyal members of the French Government to French North Africa so that they could carry on the war from there. In London he found Jean Monnet, another intensely patriotic Frenchman who wholeheartedly shared his resolve to fight on.

These two Frenchmen later became leading figures

in Common Market affairs, but in character and outlook
they could hardly have been more different. Jean Monnet
was born in 1888, and as a young man inherited a successful brandy business. He was pro-British and also pro-
American, and came to know these countries well during
his travels as a brandy salesman. He has since taken a
wide variety of jobs all over the world in business concerns
and in the organization and management of international
institutions, always working for better understanding between nations. Because Monnet is by nature so outgoing
and friendly, he is a welcome figure in many capital cities;
and because he has never been connected with any particular political party, or sought personal power, he has
no competitors and few enemies.

   In the First World War, Monnet was already working to promote Anglo-French cooperation with the United
States, and for a time he served as deputy secretary to the
League of Nations. He was disillusioned by the failure of
the League, but he never lost his vision of a united Europe.
He has an exceptional talent for bringing together, in an
atmosphere of tolerance and goodwill, people of different
nationalities and opposed political opinions. He is not
unduly starry-eyed about the difficulties of persuading
people to surrender their sovereignties and coordinate
their cultures. But he believes that if men agree to live by
the same rules, and respect the same institutions, they will
in the course of time adapt their ideas and customs to a

Jean Monnet

similar way of life. He likens this process to the development of civilization and the pattern of human behavior through the ages. Monnet admires American achievement, and he pictures a strong, united Europe able to deal with the United States on equal terms, without feeling either inferior or superior. At the age of more than eighty, his enthusiasm is as keen as ever and his grasp of international problems just as firm.

Charles de Gaulle was born in 1890 in the industrial town of Lille in northern France. He was brought up in a highly educated home with a very religious atmosphere. His father, a professor of philosophy and literature at a Jesuit college, devoted a great deal of time to the personal instruction of his own children. Charles decided on the army as a career, and passed with distinction through the Military Academy of St. Cyr. He then joined an infantry regiment commanded by Colonel (later Marshal) Philippe Pétain who for many years he greatly admired. During the First World War de Gaulle was wounded and taken prisoner at the battle of Verdun while fighting under Pétain's command, and he spent the remainder of the war in a German prison camp.

As a boy, Charles de Gaulle was exceptionally tall for his age, and he soon developed the massive build and gaunt, hawklike demeanor which have made him a conspicuous figure in any gathering. He was never easygoing or popular. He did not make friends nor seem to need them. It has been said by people who worked with him that he was always obstinate, and often right. He was just as dedicated to the idea of a united Europe as Jean Monnet. But whereas Monnet pictured a community of nations with equal status, de Gaulle's concept of an ideal Europe was an association of nations with France predominant, and the other countries clustering around, rather like chickens around the mother hen.

De Gaulle and Monnet met for the first time in London in June 1940, under the dark cloud of impending French defeat. Both men were destined, in their different ways, to play outstanding parts in European affairs. At this point they were trying desperately to stave off an armistice on German terms. As soon as de Gaulle arrived, Monnet brought him an impressive plan he had conceived, proposing the immediate formation of a single Franco-British state. At first de Gaulle was shocked at the idea, but Monnet persuaded him to present it to Winston Churchill. Together they went to see the British Prime Minister who, after considerable personal misgiving and consultation with the war cabinet, finally consented to approach the ailing French Government in a last effort to restore morale.

On June 16, both Churchill and de Gaulle outlined the plan by telephone to Paul Reynaud, the French Premier, who was then at Bordeaux. The following day de Gaulle flew out to urge his acceptance. In the name of his country, Churchill offered Reynaud the benefits of complete unity. Britain and France would no longer be two nations, but a single state. They would make a combined war effort under one war cabinet. Moreover, Britain and the Commonwealth would share resources with France in the cause of freedom. It was a unique gesture in the history of nations, but when Reynaud approached his own cabinet, they turned down the offer. They were suspicious of British motives, afraid of losing their independence, and unwilling to face the sacrifice of fighting on. As a result of the refusal, Reynaud resigned and France immediately sued for a separate peace with Germany. Two days later de Gaulle went on the air, broadcasting to the French people, telling them that he would continue the struggle and appealing to them to support him.

After this de Gaulle and Monnet went their separate ways. They never again saw eye to eye on any issue. De Gaulle remained in London as head of the Free French Resistance Movement, organizing an underground war against the Nazi occupation of his country; and planning for the hour of victory when he would return to France and take charge of the government. Monnet went to the United States and worked in Washington, always pressing the idea of greater cooperation between the United States and the nations fighting for survival against Nazi domination, and quietly pursuing his dream of European unity.

During the Second World War, London became a center for free men of many nations. Patriots escaped from countries overrun by Hitler's armies and set up headquarters under governments composed of men who refused to submit to Nazi oppression. Poles, Czechs, Yugoslavs, Greeks, Dutch, Norwegians, Belgians and Frenchmen schemed for final victory. Among them were a number of men, like Paul-Henri Spaak, who later overcame their enmity to Germany and supported the idea of German partnership in the Common Market.

De Gaulle spent an uneasy five years in England. He was passionately proud and determined at all costs not to seek favors or appear to be dependent on British help. He refused to recognize any efforts to promote resistance within France that were not under his command. He was at times indiscreet and always prickly. But he was the center of the spirit of French resistance and Churchill recognized his importance, though he often, to de Gaulle's fury, excluded him from high level meetings. It is reported that Churchill said that the heaviest cross he had to bear during these anxious years was the Cross of Lorraine—the symbol de Gaulle chose for his followers. De Gaulle was, from the very beginning of the war, opposed to any association with the United States. Churchill well knew that without American aid Britain was perilously close to defeat and he therefore worked as closely as possible with President Roosevelt. De Gaulle bitterly resented the Anglo-American accord and after the war many of these resentments lingered and later emerged as brakes and barriers to French cooperation with the United States and Britain.

Between the fall of France in June 1940 and the Japanese surrender in August 1945, the world was torn apart in a wave of destruction hitherto unknown in the history of mankind. Ever since the catastrophe, world leaders have been faced with the demanding and delicate task of picking up the broken pieces and fitting them together in a form that promises well for the future.

4

THE ROAD TO RECOVERY

On April 30, 1945 Adolf Hitler committed suicide in an air-raid shelter underneath the Chancellery in the center of Berlin. Gradually his conquests had been wrested away, and the Allied Armies had closed in on his capital from all sides. From the east, in a series of tremendous battles, the Red Army had driven the Nazi invaders back fifteen hundred miles from the city of Stalingrad on the Volga River. From the west, the British, United States and French Armies had fought their way from the Normandy beaches, across the great river barrier of the Rhine and deep into Germany. From the south, the Allied forces of many nations had advanced from Sicily up the long leg of Italy into Bavaria. At the same time, with ever increasing strength, the Allied Air Forces had pounded Germany by day and night. Many cities were in ruins, factories and shipyards at a standstill, bridges broken and roads choked with debris, and the railways reduced to lines of twisted metal.

On May 7, Admiral Doenitz, whom Hitler had

Industrial devastation in Germany

named as his successor, signed an unconditional surrender
because he had nothing left to fight with. The Nazi regime
survived its founder by just one week.

Through "blood, sweat and tears," in the famous
words of Winston Churchill, the Allies had won the war;
now they had to turn their minds from the struggle for
sheer survival to shaping a world where men could live
in peace. As early as 1941, before the United States entered the war, Winston Churchill crossed the Atlantic in
the greatest secrecy for a meeting with President Roosevelt. The two leaders conferred in a battleship off the
coast of Newfoundland, and drew up the Atlantic
Charter—a document expressing their faith in universal
liberty and in a society of nations based on the four essential freedoms: freedom of speech, freedom of worship,
freedom from want and freedom from fear.

Four months later Japanese aircraft attacked, without warning, the American naval base at Pearl Harbor in
the Pacific, and the United States joined Britain and the
Commonwealth, the Soviet Union and the Free Governments in London in their battle against Japanese aggression and Nazi tyranny.

In 1944 representatives of the United States, the
Soviet Union, Great Britain and China gathered at a
mansion called Dumbarton Oaks in Washington D.C.
for preliminary talks on planning the peace. Six months
later, in April 1945 when the war in Europe was drawing
to a close, the four nations met again at San Francisco.
This time the French also attended the conference, having
earned a place there through the performance of the

Free French Armies in liberating Western Europe, and at the insistence of Winston Churchill. The purpose of the meeting was to lay the foundations of international accord. The delegates at Dumbarton Oaks were conscious of the shortcomings and final failure of the League of Nations and determined to do better. They invited forty-five other nations to join the debate.

All of them accepted, though Poland did not attend as the country was in the throes of forming a new government. After lengthy, and at times heated, discussion the assembled nations announced the formation of the United Nations Organization and proclaimed the Charter. Foremost among the declared aims were the abolition of poverty and the promotion of peace among nations.

In the heat of battle the war aims of the Allied leaders were identical. All their available manpower and material resources were wholly committed to the cause of victory. But even before the fighting ended, Western leaders began to suspect that their peace aims differed from those of Stalin. After the German surrender, when the danger of death receded, national and political ambitions came out into the open and it was clear that the thinking of the Communists was diametrically opposed to that of the democratic nations.

On June 5, 1945 the Commanders-in-Chief of the four Allied forces—Britain, France, the Soviet Union and the United States—announced that they would take over complete control of Germany and Austria. They divided

THE ROAD TO RECOVERY

the two defeated nations into four zones of occupation, and dispatched military commanders and staffs to administer them. Berlin lay within the Soviet Zone, and the city was divided into four sectors, each one occupied by one of the victorious powers. For the time being Berlin was subject to four-power control, though later on the Communists incorporated their sector of the city into the Soviet Zone as the capital of East Germany.

With the Allied proclamation of June 1945 the German and Austrian governments ceased to exist. But whereas the Western powers declared that they would act as caretaker nations, continuing their occupation only until the Germans and Austrians had sufficiently recovered from the evils of Nazi rule to set up freely elected democratic governments, Stalin soon made it clear that he planned to keep a permanent hold on Eastern Germany. He was determined that Germany should never again unite under a single government unless the whole country turned Communist. In the meantime he organized Eastern Germany as an extension of communism, and a buffer between the Soviet Union and the rest of Europe. Moreover he stripped the country of any remaining food and machinery to compensate in some small part for the widespread devastation in Russia.

Largely owing to the alliance with America, the countries of Western Europe had triumphed over the immense military might of Nazi Germany. Five million American soldiers, sailors and airmen had fought with the British forces, and masses of tanks and aircraft, guns and ammunition, warships and landing craft, and all the other complicated paraphernalia of modern warfare had rolled off assembly lines in newly constructed factories all over North America and been ferried across the Atlantic to contribute to the victory.

But, at the end of the war, while the United States remained rich and powerful, the European nations were impoverished and confused. The order of things had changed and Britain and France no longer held important positions in world affairs. France had been defeated and occupied, Britain had spent all its gold reserves and sold out overseas investments to pay for food to keep the people alive, and arms to fight the enemy. Both countries were sandwiched between the technical leadership of the United States in the West, and a huge new and menacing Communist empire in the East.

When the Red Army expelled the Nazi forces from the countries bordering the Soviet Union, Stalin sent in Communist agents to take them over. He eliminated local leaders, abolished free elections and set up Communist puppet parliaments taking their orders from Moscow. Hungary, Rumania, Poland, Albania, and later Czechoslovakia, became satellite states under the Communist title of People's Democracies, entirely dominated by the Soviet Union. Germany was divided between East Germany, occupied by Soviet forces; and West Germany, occupied by the Americans, the British and the French.

Both Franklin Roosevelt and Winston Churchill had hoped to establish world peace by international consent in agreement with Joseph Stalin. Roosevelt died just before the German surrender, and was succeeded by Vice-President Harry Truman. In Britain, the Conservatives lost the postwar election and Winston Churchill handed over leadership to Clement Attlee, at the head of a Labour Government. Truman and Attlee were soon forced to acknowledge that it seemed hopeless to plan a peaceful future with the Communist leaders. In day-to-day diplomacy, and in the United Nations, the Soviet delegates openly opposed every measure that did not directly further Communist interests.

United States leaders soon saw the danger of a weak and destitute Europe, easy prey to Communist propaganda, and they rejected the policy of isolationism that their predecessors had adopted after the First World War. They realized that if America abandoned Europe, people who were hungry and homeless were likely to be sucked into the Soviet system from sheer desperation. So, on June 5, 1947 General George Marshall, the United States Secretary of State, made his famous speech at Harvard University, announcing the most generous and far-reaching program of voluntary aid for needy countries that the world has ever known.

The Marshall Plan, named for its author, proposed an outright gift of twelve-billion American dollars ($12,000,000,000) to the hungry and battered countries to help them to rebuild their tottering economies and enable them to plan for the future. In actual fact, when civil and military aid ended in 1966 the United States Treasury had spent ten times that sum because the bills were much bigger than estimated. The Plan was designed as a coordinated effort in which each nation pooled its resources in order to make the maximum possible contribution to European recovery, with the United States backing them up. On April 16, 1948 fifteen countries and the American, British and French commanders of the occupation zones of Germany and Austria gratefully accepted the offer and agreed to the terms of the Organization for European Economic Cooperation (OEEC), an agency set up to oversee Marshall Aid. Eventually OEEC had seventeen member states, including Greece and Turkey and every country of Western Europe except Spain, which had remained neutral during the Second World War and was therefore not eligible for postwar aid; and Finland, where the Communist Party was very powerful. Under the direction of Paul Hoffman, a distinguished writer and experienced administrator, the OEEC arranged for just distribution of its funds among the many claimants.

It appears that the Marshall Plan provided the first conflict between the European countries in favor of some form of federation, and those which stood for separate development. The federalists, headed by France, agreed with the Americans and wanted to have Marshall Aid

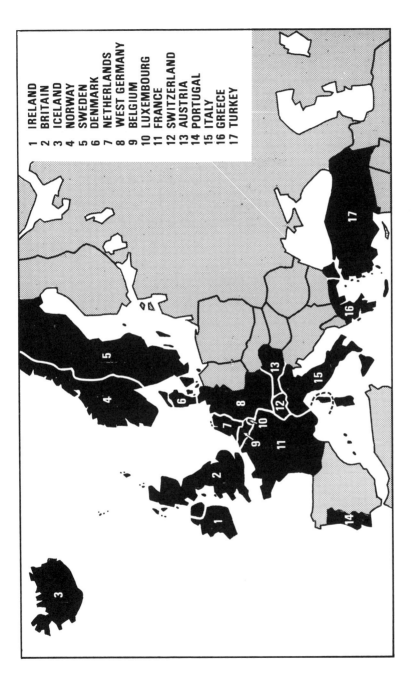

1 IRELAND
2 BRITAIN
3 ICELAND
4 NORWAY
5 SWEDEN
6 DENMARK
7 NETHERLANDS
8 WEST GERMANY
9 BELGIUM
10 LUXEMBOURG
11 FRANCE
12 SWITZERLAND
13 AUSTRIA
14 PORTUGAL
15 ITALY
16 GREECE
17 TURKEY

Marshall Aid Countries

administered by closely knit, federal-type institutions. They were opposed by Britain and the Scandinavian countries, which were prepared to cooperate in sharing out the aid, but only on condition that national governments would have the last word in deciding how the money should be spent. The anti-federalists won the battle and by this decision, Britain, through her Foreign Secretary, Ernest Bevin, was thought by many on the Continent to have struck the first blow against a united Europe.

Marshall Aid was given to both ex-allies and ex-enemies. In 1949 West Germany became an independent Federal Republic and a member of OEEC. The Federal Republic received large sums because its need was so great. In every case, Marshall Aid money was handed out as a gift instead of a loan, because it was evident that if the nations were loaded with debts the whole purpose of the project would be defeated. Moreover, the Americans gave it free of political conditions. The receiving nations were at liberty to rebuild their lives in their own way and form their own governments without external obligation. But, at the same time, the Marshall Aid planners hoped that people who were prosperous and proud of it would want to be free and therefore resist Communist pressure. And they looked ahead to the day when European recovery would lead to European unity.

In the Scandinavian countries, through Western Europe and southwards to Italy and Greece, people set to

Marshall Plan reconstruction in a French village

work to build roads and bridges, railways and airfields, factories and oil refineries, churches, schools, hospitals and houses, and marked them with the royal-blue plaque, the emblem of Marshall Aid.

The planners were prepared to help democratic and Communist countries alike, according to their needs. But Stalin turned down the offer for the Soviet Union and also prevented the People's Democracies from accepting it. There were probably two compelling reasons behind this severe decision. First, he was absolutely determined that no Communist country should receive gifts from the Western world, in case the people began to suspect that the capitalists were not quite as bad as they were painted by Party propaganda. Second, in order to claim aid, the country concerned was obliged to declare the state of its finances, and prove that the aid was really necessary. In the aftermath of the war the desolation in Russia was so great, and the future prospect so bleak, that Stalin dared not admit even to his own people what they were up against, for fear they would give way to utter despair. The only way he kept up their spirits was by telling them that countries in the West were far worse off, and that the workers were cruelly exploited and bowed down by capitalist oppression. He introduced rigid censorship and lowered what Winston Churchill called an "iron curtain," cutting off all contact between the Communist states and the West.

Under the direction of the OEEC the Marshall Plan exceeded the highest hopes and expectations of the planners, and in a few years most of the receiving countries were well on the way to recovery. In 1961, after thirteen years' work, the OEEC had accomplished its goals and was succeeded by the OECD—the Organization for Economic Cooperation and Development. By this time the member countries had reached a level of prosperity they had never known before, and inter-European trade was booming. It had been proved that European economic cooperation was a paying proposition for all concerned.

While Marshall Aid was getting under way, thoughts of political partnership were in the minds of many men. In 1948 distinguished delegates from all over Europe met at The Hague, the capital of the Netherlands, to pave the way to further union. They were eminent statesmen, disciplined by war and sickened with strife.

They arrived with high hopes and noble ambitions, and made eloquent speeches, for they genuinely believed in the splendid future of a united Europe. Winston Churchill said: "I hope to see a Europe where men and women of every country will think as much of being European as of belonging to their native land and wherever they go in this wide domain will truly feel 'Here I am at home.' " He, and other speakers who expressed similar sentiments, received tumultuous applause from the assembled company.

As an outcome of the Congress of The Hague, the nations formed the Council of Europe, and agreed to set up headquarters at Strasbourg. No other city had changed hands so often after Franco-German wars, or aroused such intense feelings of animosity between the French

Headquarters of the Council of Europe and meeting place of the European Parliament in Strasbourg

and German people. Therefore the choice of Strasbourg as a meeting ground for European discussion stressed their desire to bury the past and work together for the future. The building which housed the Council was symbolically christened *La Maison de l'Europe*.

In May 1949 representatives of ten countries attended the opening ceremony and elected the Belgian Prime Minister Paul-Henri Spaak as their president. In the following decade, eight additional nations joined the Council of Europe so that today the flags of Austria, Belgium, Britain, Cyprus, Denmark, France, Western Germany, Greece, Iceland, Ireland, Italy, Luxembourg, Malta, the Netherlands, Norway, Sweden, Switzerland and Turkey fly before the building.

The Council of Europe is an independent assembly, not to be confused with the European Parliament which was founded later and now shares the same premises. On the political side, it has provided a forum where men and women from the eighteen nations can meet once a month to exchange ideas, propose reforms, air their grievances and explore the possibilities of closer cooperation. In a practical way, it has given help and advice in many different aspects of European activity. Special committees study the major problems of refugees, communications, health, art, social services, and the multitude of minor problems that crop up in day-to-day life. The Council has not proved itself a powerful force in European affairs, but nevertheless it promotes friendship and does useful work.

The Council of Europe is also working with the European Council of Ministers of Education, and other academic authorities, to standardize university degrees all over the Continent. When they succeed in fixing a general standard of higher education, students will be able to earn degrees and diplomas in one country, and practice their profession in another without the delay and anxiety

of taking more examinations in order to gain fresh qualifications. This is a measure which will encourage young
graduates to work outside their own countries, and could
lead to a tremendous increase in understanding and
goodwill.

5

COLD WAR BETWEEN EAST AND WEST

WITH THE ADVENT of Marshall Aid, conditions in the Western zones of Germany began to improve, though the Soviet zone was still poverty-stricken. As chaos gave way to law and order, and the wheels of industry began to turn, the American, British and French military commanders saw that the time was approaching when the West Germans and the Austrians would be ready to take over their own governments and handle their own affairs.

The attitude of the people of the defeated nations was less bitter than after the First World War. They were so thankful when the bombing ended that they viewed the occupation almost with relief. As they moved into new or patched-up homes and found jobs in civilian life, they saw that though the Allied authorities came as conquerors, they were staying to help. Many Germans were satisfied to be rid of Nazi rule at almost any cost, and they began to look to the future with hope and some degree of confidence.

But, despite the obvious progress, German finances

Occupation Zones of Germany and Austria

were in trouble. At the end of the war, when the country was in ruins and trade at a standstill, the value of the mark had once more dropped to practically nothing. It was hardly worthwhile for people to work because they could buy so little with their wages, and they made more money bartering goods on the black market. This illegal trading was a holdover from the war when everything was in short supply, and ordinary articles such as shoes, cigarettes and soap had an entirely artificial value. The Western powers decided on a currency reform to strengthen the mark so that the new republic would start off on a sound financial basis and the people could earn a good living. They warned Stalin of their intentions, and offered to mint the new marks for the Soviet zone at the same time as their own.

True to his postwar policy, Stalin firmly refused to come to any form of agreement with the West. Angered by the knowledge that the currency reform would accelerate recovery and create an even greater contrast between conditions in East and West Germany, he planned a harsh reprisal. On June 20, 1948 the Allied officials closed the banks in order to introduce the currency reform, and three days later the Russian military commander ordered the manager of the power station in the Soviet sector of Berlin to cut off the current which supplied the rest of the city with almost all its electricity.

The following day Soviet guards closed every road, rail and water route connecting Berlin with West Germany. The Americans, British and French had airports in their sectors of the city and the right to approach them by specified air corridors. They were accustomed to flying in people, mail and some perishable goods, but they transported all the main supplies of food, fuel and merchandise by truck, train and barge through the Soviet zone. They suddenly found themselves without heating or lighting, running short of the necessities of life and responsible for the survival of two million Germans who lived in West Berlin.

Stalin hoped, by means of the blockade, to drive the Allies out of the city and to starve the German population until they submitted to Communist rule. But he misjudged the character of his opponents. When the first shock was over, they took up the challenge and set out to cope with the crisis. The British and the Americans had between them about a hundred transport aircraft based in West Germany. They began flying in a few tons of food every day, more as a gesture of defiance than as a real rescue campaign. But when it became clear that Stalin intended to continue the blockade, they stepped up the airlift until it became a major operation. At first the British took the lead as they were nearer the scene of action, but soon the Americans flew fleets of aircraft across the Atlantic and enlarged their bases in Britain and West Germany. At the end of three months they were carrying twice the load of the British.

It was dangerous and exhausting flying along narrow

corridors and landing on overcrowded runways. But the air crews and ground staff were on duty day and night, and the Berliners worked with them, enlarging the airports and unloading the supplies. It was an epic of courage, resolution and good organization. Morale was high and relations friendly between the Western Allies and the people of West Berlin. When the Berliners held their first postwar election not a single Communist candidate won a seat on the city council. By the spring of 1949 the airlift was running like clockwork, Berlin was receiving plentiful supplies, and Stalin saw that he was beaten. But it is dangerous for dictators to admit defeat, and it was difficult for him to save face. Finally, through secret talks carried on with the help of the United Nations, Stalin reached a compromise with the Western powers which enabled him to lift the blockade without making a public confession of failure.

Already a stream of anti-Western propaganda was pouring out of the Kremlin, and a Cold War of angry words separated the Communists from the rest of the world. But the Berlin blockade had a profound effect on East–West relations and the future of Europe, for it probably did more than any other Soviet action to highlight the threat of Communism, draw the European countries together and bring the United States to the point of signing a peacetime military alliance to defend the West against Communist aggression.

In March 1948 Britain, France, Belgium, the Netherlands and Luxembourg had signed the Brussels Treaty, a defensive alliance to coordinate military policy and make the most of their limited supplies of arms and equipment. When the five countries got down to a detailed estimate of their united resources, they soon realized that they were helpless in the face of Soviet might and they sent off an urgent appeal to the United States for help. By this time President Harry Truman and Secretary of State George Marshall were on their guard, watching intently Stalin's every move. They had been compelled to stand by idly while the Soviet Union broke the promises Stalin had made to Western leaders during the war, and annexed part of Finland and the three Baltic states of Latvia, Lithuania and Estonia. And they had witnessed with profound disapproval the establishment of Communist regimes in Poland, East Germany, Hungary, Rumania, Albania, and finally in Czechoslovakia. These regimes were imposed without the consent of the people, and most of them are maintained by force. When Stalin discarded all pretense of friendship with the West and blockaded Berlin, the anxiety of the Americans deepened.

Their immediate response to the European plea was a turning point in world affairs. It was a direct reversal of former American policy and a contradiction of repeatedly declared American aims. For the first time in the history of the nation the United States Government formed a defensive alliance with Canada and a number of European powers, thus undertaking a military com-

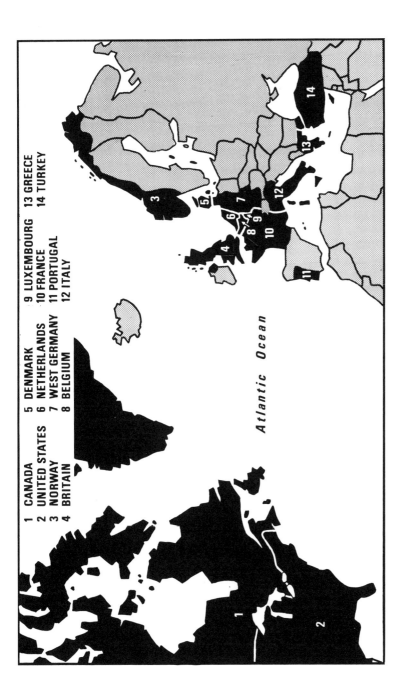

1 CANADA	5 DENMARK	9 LUXEMBOURG	13 GREECE
2 UNITED STATES	6 NETHERLANDS	10 FRANCE	14 TURKEY
3 NORWAY	7 WEST GERMANY	11 PORTUGAL	
4 BRITAIN	8 BELGIUM	12 ITALY	

Members of the North Atlantic Treaty Organization

mitment, outside the American continent, in peacetime.

On April 4, 1949 representatives of eleven nations gathered in Washington, D.C. to set up the North Atlantic Treaty Organization, now generally referred to as NATO. This organization aimed at the creation of a collective system of defense against outside aggression. According to Article Five of the Treaty, governments agreed that "an armed attack against any of them would be considered as an attack directed against all the parties."

The countries that signed the momentous document were: the original five of the Brussels Treaty, Britain, France, Belgium, the Netherlands and Luxembourg; the European states of Italy, Portugal, Norway and Denmark; and the United States and Canada. In 1951 Greece and Turkey joined NATO, and in 1955 the Federal Republic of Germany became a full member, bringing the total membership up to fourteen.

A few days after the formation of the Atlantic Alliance, Stalin lifted the Berlin blockade and the Western Allies resumed the use of the normal traffic routes to the city. The Cold War continued, but the Western world had expressed its determination to stand together, and the United States had taken on the main responsibility for European survival.

In the Western zones of Germany the currency reform was working miracles, industry was booming and plans were going ahead for an independent state in West Germany.

6

THE NEW LOOK IN EUROPE

WHILE THE PACE of European production speeded up, the long-standing enmity between France and Germany died down.

West German leaders bitterly resented the enforced division of their territory between the Soviet Union and the West. But they decided to accept the Allied proposal to set up a republic in the Western half of the country because they saw that the only other alternative was to hold out for German unity on an all-or-nothing basis and risk having no independent state at all.

In 1948 during the Berlin blockade a parliamentary council met, under the chairmanship of Konrad Adenauer, to draft a Constitution for the new republic. As Nazism faded, new political parties arose and old ones revived. Konrad Adenauer became head of the Christian Democratic Union, the CDU, a new party formed of both Protestants and Catholics. Ever since the Reformation in the sixteenth century, German Protestants and Roman Catholics had been divided in their outlook and political opinions. But after the Second World War the wars of religion seemed very remote, and the wars of power politics very recent. The CDU was a Christian coalition of the two churches, and it attracted many supporters who decided to sink their religious differences for the sake of a well-balanced government. The CDU stood for democratic rule and the reconstruction of West Germany through a rapid return to a sound economy.

In August 1949 free elections were held in West Germany and the people voted for a parliament, or *Bundestag,* to take over from the occupation authorities the government of the newly proclaimed Federal Republic of Germany. When the Bundestag assembled to choose its ministers, Konrad Adenauer was elected Chancellor by a majority of one vote over the candidates of all other parties. The seat of the federal parliament was established at Bonn, which lies on the banks of the Rhine, fifteen miles south of Cologne. Berlin remained the official capital of all Germany, though it was· a city divided between East and West and surrounded on all sides by Soviet-controlled territory.

In reply to the foundation of the Federal Republic, Stalin announced the formation of the Democratic Republic of Germany in the Soviet zone, under the nominal leadership of a Moscow-trained German Communist named Walter Ulbricht. Stalin then created an armed barrier between East and West Germany by wiring off a three-mile-wide stretch of country separating the Democratic Republic from the Federal Republic. He ordered the Red Army to plant the area with mines, and posted armed guards along the length of the frontier. In 1961 Nikita Khrushchev, Stalin's successor, built a concrete wall around the Soviet sector of Berlin to prevent people from escaping from the stagnant poverty and political pressure of East Germany to the growing prosperity and political freedom of the West.

There had already been an important movement toward integrating West Germany with other countries in Western Europe. In 1950 Robert Schuman, the French Foreign Minister, made a bold but carefully considered move in the direction of Franco-German friendship. He delivered a declaration proposing that France and Germany, the main producers of coal and steel in Europe, should pool their production. At the same time he invited other European countries to join the merger. This plan, known as the Schuman Plan, bears the name of the French Foreign Minister; but it is common knowledge that it was inspired by Jean Monnet, and that he had a large hand in shaping the policy. The Plan was a creation of Schuman and Monnet and it contained many of their ideas and objectives. Germany accepted the Schuman Plan. So did Italy under the guidance of the Prime Minister Alcide de Gasperi, leader of the Italian Christian Democratic Party, and the most able statesman who emerged after the fall of Mussolini and the return of the Italian people to democratic government. Belgium went in on the advice of Paul-Henri Spaak. The Netherlands and Luxembourg had already formed a customs union with Belgium, under the name Benelux, by which they hoped to abolish all frontier duties between the three countries. The Common Market fitted their ideas, and they came in too.

These were the internationally minded Six that later formed the European Economic Community. In 1951, by the Treaty of Paris, they adopted the terms of the European Coal and Steel Community, the ECSC. They set up headquarters in Luxembourg, and Jean Monnet himself became head of the organization for the first three years of its life.

At this critical time in the growth of European integration Jean Monnet was in charge of French economic planning. He had feelings of great friendship for the British, and he had always assumed that they would take an active part in movements toward European unity. When Schuman announced the coal and steel plan, Monnet flew to London to deliver a personal invitation to the British Government. When he arrived he found Prime Minister Clement Attlee and Foreign Minister Ernest Bevin stubbornly opposed to handing over control of British coal and steel to a Higher Authority situated on the Continent. In the 1950's British leaders, both Labour and Conservative, were living in a political period that was already past. Their thinking dated from the days before the First World War when the British Isles were

Robert Schuman signs the Treaty of Paris

the center of a rich and immensely powerful empire. Britain's politicians still pictured their line of defense against a possible aggressor on the other side of the English Channel instead of on the frontier of East and West Germany where it really lay. They could not see that the proud slogan "The sun never sets on the Union Jack" no longer held good. India had already claimed its independence, the African colonies were following suit, and Britain was not strong enough to stand in splendid isolation from her neighbors. But the government had not faced up to the need for cooperation with Western Europe, and Bevin refused the French invitation to join the Coal and Steel Community. Monnet returned to France bitterly disappointed.

The immense importance of the ECSC lay in the fact that, in those days, nations needed both coal and steel to go to war. Coal was then—and is still, to a lesser extent—an essential driving force in industry. Moreover, the most recent and sensational scientific discoveries have not yet found a substitute to enable armament factories to turn out weapons without steel. Therefore, it followed that when the French and German governments agreed to abide by the rules of the European Coal and Steel Community by which they handed over their coal and steel industries to a form of European management, they entered into a pact which made it almost impossible for the two countries to go to war against one another.

The French proposal and the German acceptance of

opening the way for a common market

the Schuman Plan, and their joint signatures with those
of Italy, Belgium, the Netherlands and Luxembourg, of
the Treaty of Paris, opened the way to the Common
Market and raised hopes of future political union. It was
a remarkable achievement by French and German leaders
that only five years after the two countries were fighting
the most devastating war of all time, their people were
prepared to scrap their pride and bury their differences in
order to work together for permanent peace.

It is doubtful if the ECSC could have come into being
so quickly without the sound political judgment and fore-
sight of Konrad Adenauer, the newly elected, elderly
Chancellor of the Federal Republic. He was seventy-two
years old when he took on the heavy responsibilities of
high office. But his mind was clear, his energy unbounded,
his experience invaluable, and he never lacked the courage to carry out his convictions.

Adenauer spent his boyhood and received his education in a devout Catholic environment in the Rhineland
city of Cologne. Though the Rhineland was part of
Prussia, because the people were Catholic they looked to
Rome and Paris for leadership, as well as to Berlin. In
his youth he did not take part in the goose-stepping
parades, or absorb the spirit of rampant militarism of the
Prussian capital.

Adenauer loved his homeland, and was devoted to
the city of Cologne with its fine bridges and majestic
cathedral. He trained as a lawyer with a view to entering

the civil service, and soon after he received his degree he was elected to the city council. In 1917, at the height of the First World War, Adenauer became chief *Bürgermeister,* or mayor, of Cologne. In the aftermath of German defeat he struggled to rebuild Rhineland industry and restore morale. When Hitler came to power he removed the Burgomeister from public office. Adenauer was twice arrested for his independent views and was very fortunate to escape the fate of most political prisoners during the Nazi regime.

After the German collapse in 1945, Cologne lay within the British occupation zone. The British military authorities, looking for politicians free from the taint of Nazism, reinstated Adenauer. But he proved too obstinate and outspoken; they could not work with him and soon appointed a less dynamic and more cooperative mayor.

As the time came to draw up a constitution and rule of basic law for West Germany, Adenauer wholeheartedly supported the Allied proposal of a Federal Republic. Officially, the Christian Democrats refused to recognize the existence of a separate state in East Germany. But Adenauer had witnessed two wars, and put the importance of peaceful links with the West before the campaign for the reunification of his country. When he became Chancellor he did not conceal his resolve to work with the United States and mobilize Western strength in order to promote European unity. He was also determined to wipe out the deep-seated hostility between Germany and

France, and find a way to establish Franco-German friendship. He accepted the somewhat limited powers the Allies offered his government because he felt sure that the Communist menace was growing, and that the Federal Republic would inevitably hold a valuable frontline position in the defense system of Western Europe, and thus regain recognition and self-respect.

At the end of the Second World War the victorious Allies demanded total disarmament and the dismantling of any arms factories which had not already been destroyed. The Germans willingly accepted the ban; they did not want to rearm for they saw the advantages of using their scanty resources and their share of Marshall Aid for the kind of reconstruction that would put the country on its feet. They realized that it would help greatly, when they were competing in world markets, if they could concentrate on cars, tractors, sewing machines, tools, cameras and optical instruments, instead of wasting their money and manpower on an arms race.

But Adenauer looked ahead to the time when, of necessity, German military divisions would be called upon to take their place in a European system of defense, closely integrated into a European Community.

In 1952, a year after the Six had signed the Treaty of Paris, the European Coal and Steel Community came into being. The terms had been set by statesmen who were both peaceloving and practical, and they created an organization which had never existed in Europe before.

Jean Monnet sets off the first European Coal and Steel Community blast furnace

Germany was the largest producer of coal among the Six, with a network of mines in the industrial area of the Ruhr; France was second, with mines in the northeast and in Lorraine. The Coal and Steel Community abolished trade barriers, such as frontier tariffs, and opened up the flow of trade between the nations. The High Authority supervised the whole production and distribution of coal and steel, and abolished the big trusts which had dominated the industry and at times made it almost impossible for the countries which had to import coal and steel to buy what they needed at reasonable prices.

The Coal and Steel Community experts saw that there would inevitably be changes in the industrial pattern of Europe, and recognized the need to ensure that these changes should not occur at the expense of the workers. They therefore set up an organization to retrain workers if their jobs folded up, and guaranteed them an income during the retraining. As the use of oil has increased, the demand for coal has diminished, and the Coal and Steel Community has taken on the task of resettling miners in new areas and new countries and giving them the qualifications to make a living. The retraining staff gives would-be migrants advice on job opportunities and warns them against regions where the prospects are poor. It costs about $2,000 a year to carry out the changeover of a single worker, and the cost is shared equally between the funds of the Coal and Steel Community—which are

The European Coal and Steel Community at work

collected in taxes on the turnover of the firms administered by the High Authority—and contributions from the
governments concerned. It is evident that if workers do
not have to suffer distress and uncertainty in changing
their jobs, and can look forward to a secure living in new
surroundings, they will probably be enthusiastic supporters of technical progress.

The members of the High Authority gathered at the
Coal and Steel Community headquarters in Luxembourg
for consultation, striving to increase efficiency, pep up
production and promote prosperity. They conferred with
Trade Union leaders, examining wage claims and making
provision for greater safety at work. The success of the
coal and steel merger was a pointer to the possibilities of
European integration and a landmark in peacetime
planning.

7

NO PLACE FOR A EUROPEAN ARMY

By 1950 the nations of Western Europe were united in two ways: by thankfulness in their growing prosperity at home, and by renewed fear of Soviet expansion—for in this year the Communists started a war in the Far Eastern country of Korea. The origins of the Korean War date from the Japanese surrender in 1945 when the Russians, who had just declared war on Japan, entered Korea from the north; and American forces, who had been fighting in the Pacific, moved up from the south to take over the country. They met halfway up the Korean peninsula, on the geographical meridian of the thirty-eighth parallel which became an artificial frontier separating the Communist-controlled state of North Korea from the independent republic of South Korea.

Before dawn on June 25, 1950 North Korean troops, well-equipped with Russian arms, crossed the thirty-eighth parallel and set out to conquer the whole country. The South Koreans instantly appealed to the United Nations. As the Soviet delegates were absent, the Security Council condemned the invasion and called on the North Koreans to withdraw. As the North Koreans continued their advance, the United States proposed that the United Nations should form an international force to protect South Korea.

During the next three years a United Nations army under United States command fought a costly war, first against the North Koreans and later against crack Chinese regiments dispatched by Mao Tse-tung. Sixteen member-countries of the United Nations took part in the conflict, but the Americans provided more than half the men, money and materials, and suffered by far the greatest loss.

When the United States Government was confronted by the grim prospect of providing the main contribution to contain Communism in the Far East, the nation was already heavily committed to the defense of Europe. The Chiefs-of-Staff settled down to some serious rethinking of their obligations. They decided that the European nations must take on more responsibility for their own defense in the event of a Soviet attack; and they urged that the newly independent Federal Republic of Germany be rearmed to strengthen the Atlantic Alliance. Though he did not hold any official government position, Jean Monnet was still a most important figure in French planning. He was opposed to the American demand, but he saw that the European nations were not in a position to refuse it. Therefore he prepared a plan for the rearming of West Germany in a way which he trusted would be acceptable on both sides of the Atlantic. As a result of Monnet's work, in October 1950 René Pleven, the French Premier, proposed the formation of a European Army that would include German contingents. This was a follow-up of an idea outlined by Winston Churchill at Strasbourg, for a force to be known as the European Defense Community, recruited from the nations of Western Europe. All the units of this international army would serve under a single high command, bear a single banner, be armed with standardized weapons and wear the same uniform. Monnet considered that under these circumstances the Germans would have no national identity, so they would not be a danger to their neighbors.

The European nations adopted the idea of a European Army and proceeded to draft the details. The project suffered a sharp setback when Winston Churchill, who had become head of a Conservative government, ignored his previous suggestion and refused to participate for fear that Britain would be sucked into a federal Europe. The Germans themselves were reluctant to rearm. They had learned the lesson of defeat and had had their fill of fighting. Moreover they were growing more prosperous each year and hoped to continue on the same course.

But Adenauer saw that rearmament was inevitable if his country was going to take a respected place in the Western world. He consented to join the European Army

Konrad Adenauer

only on the condition that the Federal Republic of Germany stood as a wholly independent nation, on an equal footing with the other members of the Atlantic Alliance.

The negotiations continued for over three years, while important changes took place in world leadership. Stalin died and was succeeded by Nikita Khrushchev, and General Eisenhower was elected to the presidency of the United States by a large majority. In 1953 the Korean War ended in a compromise which reestablished the frontier between North and South Korea at the thirty-eighth parallel.

Finally, the completed draft plan for the European Army was ready for ratification. The French had had a rapid succession of governments and the country was in a state of uncertainty and unrest. The tension at home was heightened by a war of rebellion in the French Far-Eastern colony of Indochina which ended in a decisive French defeat. After their triumph, the Indochinese people broke away from French rule and proclaimed an independent republic under the name of Vietnam. In France, Pierre Mendès France, a forceful and determined lawyer, had become Premier. He presented the draft to his partners in the European Defense Community who were all prepared to accept it, not only as a military measure, but also as a step toward full federal union. The meeting ended in disastrous anticlimax for the French, who had originated the plan and nursed it for four years, refused to ratify it. On August 30, 1954 the French Assembly turned it down. The members of the government who were pro-de Gaulle refused to contemplate German rearmament at any price, and the Communist members disapproved of a measure which would offend the Soviet Union. It was an unexpected and shattering blow to the prospect of European unity.

Alcide de Gasperi, many times Prime Minister and head of the Italian Christian Democratic Party, had worked wholeheartedly for European integration. He never wavered in his conviction that the closer the countries came together, the stronger they would be. De Gasperi had taken part in the planning for the Coal and Steel Community, and he was strongly in favor of a European Army. He died of a heart attack shortly after he received the news that the French had opposed the plan.

A few months after the failure to set up a European Army, Britain concluded an agreement with the six members of the Coal and Steel Community which they called the Western European Union, or WEU. By the terms of WEU the seven countries agreed to cooperate on the limitation of armaments, and to review the whole European political and economic situation. At the same time Britain promised to keep army and airforce units on the Continent until the end of the twentieth century. In response to this assurance, and as a result of an agreement signed in Paris in the autumn of 1954 whereby Western Germany undertook not to produce any form of nuclear weapon, France consented to German rearmament. In

May 1955 a national German Army, supplied largely with American arms and equipment, but commanded by German officers, joined the North Atlantic Treaty Organization. It was a very different force from the former German Army for it was composed of some regular soldiers and some national servicemen—civilians in uniform who joined because they had to, but did not regard the army as a glorious career. So far German divisions have done the job that has been demanded of them without any show of aggression or violent militarism.

The announcement of German membership in NATO caused a swift reaction in Moscow. Khrushchev had viewed the decision to rearm the Germans with the utmost disapproval and distrust. When on May 9, 1955 the Federal Republic was granted equal status with the other nations of the Atlantic Alliance, Khrushchev pronounced it a threat to international peace. Five days later, as an act of retaliation and a deterrent to a further build-up of the Atlantic Alliance, the Soviet Union concluded a military pact with the People's Democracies. On May 14, in Warsaw, the Polish capital, representatives of the Soviet Union, Albania, Bulgaria, Czechoslovakia, East Germany, Hungary, Poland and Rumania signed a treaty of mutual defense providing for a united force under Soviet supreme command. The terms of the Warsaw Pact committed the eight nations to go to war if any one of them was attacked during the next twenty years; and they also gave the Soviet Union the right to station Red

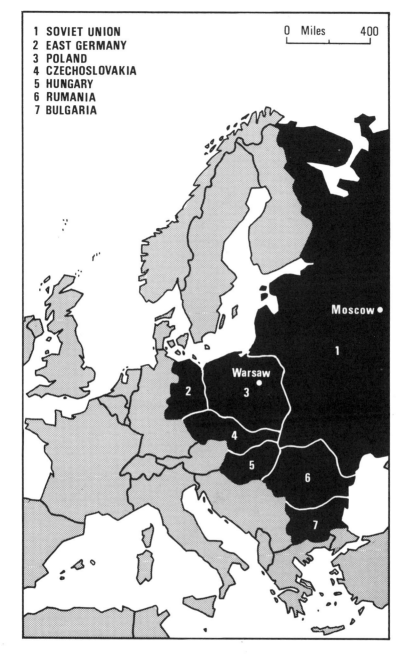

1 SOVIET UNION
2 EAST GERMANY
3 POLAND
4 CZECHOSLOVAKIA
5 HUNGARY
6 RUMANIA
7 BULGARIA

0   Miles   400

Moscow

Warsaw

Warsaw Pact Countries

Army troops on the territory of the other member states. It soon became clear that the treaty had a double purpose, for it served as a bargaining point in Soviet dealings with the West, and it tightened the Communist hold on Eastern Europe. Shortly afterwards Albania withdrew from the treaty obligations; but the other satellite states were powerless to resist Soviet pressure, and the Warsaw Pact intensified the existing hatred of Communist rule which burst out in open rebellion in Hungary and industrial riots in Poland in the following year.

8

THE MAKING OF THE COMMON MARKET

THOUGH THE COLLAPSE of the campaign for a European Army hit the spirit of European unity a hard blow, it failed to kill it. Inspired by the constant resolution of Jean Monnet and his many young followers who had grown up with the ideal of a federal Europe and now held important political jobs in their respective countries, the Six started to move forward once more toward their common goal. Less than a year after the adverse decision of the French Assembly, these true "Europeans" launched a new round of talks on closer working relations leading to firmer friendship.

Within the framework of the Atlantic Alliance, protected by the shield of United States nuclear power, the members of the European Coal and Steel Community were better off than they had ever been before. Bankers and businessmen, economic planners and politicians were all eager to tighten the links which were standing them in such good stead, and the United States enthusiastically supported any action which increased European strength and efficiency. The American Government was deeply committed to upholding the Atlantic Alliance. It was a considerable drain on the American treasury, and the leaders of both political parties were wise enough to see that if the sales of German Volkswagens and cameras, French wine and fashions and Italian machinery created prosperity at home, these countries would be in a position to build a solid bulwark against Communism.

In June 1955 the Foreign Ministers of the European Coal and Steel Community countries gathered at the ancient city of Messina, situated in Sicily on the straits which divide the island from Italy, to explore the prospects of closer cooperation. The British Government was also invited to send a Foreign Minister but Anthony Eden, who had recently succeeded Winston Churchill as Prime Minister, did not think the occasion was sufficiently important. He dispatched a Mr. Bretherton, an official from the Board of Trade, to report on the conference. Eden evidently regarded the Messina meeting as a routine discussion on commerce and customs duties, rather than as an approach to vital European relationships. He soon recalled Bretherton to resume his duties at the Board of Trade, while the Six went on from strength to strength.

After the initial discussions at Messina on the formation of a European Economic Community, a high-powered and intelligent group of European statesmen and economists from the Coal and Steel Community countries

Paul-Henri Spaak

president
of the Council of
Europe 1949

gathered in Belgium where they conferred in a secluded castle, the Chateau du Val Duchesse, near Brussels. Under the able chairmanship of Paul-Henri Spaak, they continued their discussions for nearly a year.

Jean Monnet had just resigned his post at the European Coal and Steel Community in order to form an Action Committee to promote European unity. The Committee was made up of representatives of the main European political parties—with the exception of the Communists and the Gaullists—and of the leaders of the Trade Union federations. Through these widespread contacts, Jean Monnet was able to keep in close touch with political and industrial leaders throughout Europe, and influence their thinking. Through the years the Action Committee has issued a series of declarations directed toward the establishment of closer union and of good relations with the United States and Britain, and toward widening the scope and strengthening the authority of the European Communities. He took no official part in the committee meetings at the Chateau du Val Duchesse, but he was always in the background, available for calm counsel and invaluable in finding a way through the maze of conflicting national interests and the personal disputes that, from time to time, threatened to hold up the proceedings. Prominent on the committee was Professor Walter Hallstein, a German lawyer and politician, and a magnificent administrator, who later became the first president of the European Economic Community Commission. Hallstein was also highly experienced in foreign affairs and a close friend of Chancellor Adenauer. Another brilliant member of the group was the Frenchman Pierre

Uri, an economist and writer, and a convinced European in the Community sense of the word.

In May 1956 the Spaak Committee produced a re-markably clear and well-reasoned report which laid down the foundations of the Common Market. The declared aims were the achievement of political unity through a working economic partnership. The immediate goal was the formation of a customs union abolishing frontier duties between the Six, which would come into operation in January 1970. Though the short-term program of the Spaak Committee was practical, it was inspired by the idealism of the men who had taken on the task of steering Europe toward total unity.

Once the Foreign Ministers of the Six countries ac-cepted the substance of the report, they asked the same committee to draft a formal treaty for official signature. The British took no part in the preparation of the Treaty of Rome. They cold-shouldered the proceedings, because they did not want to give up their traditional independ-ence, and also because they were convinced that when it came to the point the French Assembly would refuse to sign in just the same way that, at the last minute, they had turned against the formation of the European Army.

However, in 1956 two disturbing events took place which brought home the European lack of direction and showed up European weakness.

The first crisis arose in October when a war,

which had been brewing since the 1948 partition of Palestine and the formation of a Jewish state, broke out between Israel and Egypt. Britain and France warned that they would move in to protect the international waterway of the Suez Canal if the Arabs and Israelis did not take their forces ten miles clear of it. As the war went on, the RAF bombed Egyptian airfields and an Anglo-French force landed in Egypt. This action aroused bitter conflict in Europe and it was condemned by an overwhelming majority in the United Nations. Confronted by hostile world opinion, the British and French forces were compelled to withdraw most ignominiously.

In the same month, in the Communist-controlled People's Democracy of Hungary, patriots rebelled against Soviet restraint and oppression. They built barricades in the streets of Budapest to defend themselves against reprisals by the local police and the Warsaw Pact occupation forces. By this time Khrushchev had opened some chinks in the Iron Curtain and appeared to favor cooperation with the West; but he still ruled the countries within the Soviet sphere by force and fear. He sent Red Army tanks to Budapest to shoot down the rebels and restore control. The Western world was shocked and indignant; but, short of embarking on a third world war, they were powerless to intervene. All they could do was register a united protest in the name of common humanity and the cause of freedom.

The signing of the Rome Treaties, March 25, 1957

Shaken by these crises, in March 1957 the Foreign Ministers of France, Germany, Belgium, Italy, the Netherlands and Luxembourg assembled in Italy to sign the two Treaties of Rome, committing their countries to work together for peace and prosperity through industrial, agricultural and nuclear accord. The secretariat of the Spaak committee drew up the terms of the treaties in four languages: French, German, Dutch and Italian—the four major languages of the Six.

The ultimate object of the men most concerned with the establishment of the European Economic Community was political union; but the actual terms of the Treaty of Rome which led to the formation of the European Economic Community were less ambitious. Their aim was to set up an organization for a trade area where the member countries could buy and sell without the hindrance of customs formalities. Paul-Henri Spaak and his colleagues planned an extension of the principle of the Coal and Steel Community to enable the Six to set targets for the expansion of their industry and agriculture. They did not try to make hard and fast rules; nor dictate to manufacturers and farmers how they should distribute food, raw materials, machinery, cars, television sets, tractors, clothes and all the other things that are in daily demand. The members of the Spaak Committee considered that these decisions should be made by individual firms and farms, to stimulate healthy competition. Their aim was to set up an apparatus whereby the new Community institutions could work out common policies, and could also confer with government experts on economic and social problems. They explored ways of coordinating the legal systems of the Six to form a single code of Community law to be applied by governments and law courts, and in civil administration. They also looked ahead to the time when the Community could harmonize the conduct of business companies and integrate the various systems of transport and communication.

In the deliberations at Brussels the committee also provided for the free movement of money, so that private individuals or firms with funds to invest could use them where the opportunities were greatest. They hoped, for instance, that a German industrialist would be able to build a factory in Italy where there is surplus labor, and an Italian firm would be free to amalgamate with a French one for their mutual profit.

The architects of the Treaty of Rome, like those of the Treaty of Paris, faced up to the family problems of keeping pace with modern industry in an international community. They saw that when new industries developed there would probably be more jobs than workers, and when outdated industries declined there would certainly be more workers than jobs. The articles of the Treaty allowed for the flow of workers from one industry to another, and granted them equal rights and social security if they moved to a new country. And they also took into consideration the necessity of starting up new industries, resettling and retraining workers, providing them with houses and educating their children.

The supporters of the Common Market hoped to improve the standard of living for all the people of all the

Mass production in the European Economic Community

member nations, so that they could have better homes, more to eat, finer schools, widespread social services and, above all, greater security. They hoped to create conditions where nations would grow rich through harmonious effort, and the prosperity of one would contribute to the well-being of the rest. Scientists and scholars, bankers and industrialists, engineers, builders, architects and artists, farmers and merchants and members of all the other trades and professions would have a chance to get together to display their skills and take home new knowledge and the fruits of other people's experience.

The Treaty of Rome aimed at controlling trade within the Community, and also at establishing a trading policy toward the outside world, with a special relationship between the Six and their overseas possessions. At the time of the negotiations France was an important empire with territories all over the world, and fourteen colonies in Africa alone. Belgium also had African colonies, including the vast Congo. But the era of white supremacy was ending, and by 1960 all the French and Belgian territories in Africa had declared their independence from colonial rule.

These new nations were underdeveloped and poor. Their survival depended on finding European markets for their cocoa, coffee, cotton, groundnuts, oil, bananas, hardwood and other tropical products. Moreover, this trade with Africa worked both ways, for European manufacturers sold their goods to African buyers and granted them favorable terms.

The Treaty of Rome had envisaged the continuation of some sort of special economic relationship with African territories, and in 1958 the Six signed the first Association Convention to cover a five-year period. In 1963 they extended the agreement by signing the Yaoundé Convention with eighteen African republics, a convention which was renewed on July 1, 1969. In 1966 the previously-British colony of Nigeria also signed an agreement of association with the Six, adding another 55 million Africans to the 65 million already linked with the Community countries. In 1968 the three East African republics of Kenya, Tanzania and Uganda signed the Arusha Agreement, and have since applied to the Six for technical aid—the first African states to do so. European leaders felt that it was important to keep up their trade connection in Africa so that new states would not be left out of Common Market prosperity, and also to preserve a cultural relationship which had grown up in colonial days.

When the Foreign Ministers of the Six gathered in Rome in March 1957 to agree on the framework for the European Economic Community, they signed a second treaty setting up a separate, but closely related, organization—the European Atomic Energy Community, or Euratom. They had in fact begun to explore the possibilities of pooling nuclear energy almost before they got down

A meeting of the representatives of the Associated African Countries

to serious work on the project of economic unity, and the
two schemes had advanced side by side.

Industry was already expanding rapidly and the
leaders of the Six foresaw a quickening of the pace as a
result of Common Market opportunities. But there was
still a postwar shortage of fuel and power, and most European treasuries were too low in funds to buy sufficient

quantities of overseas oil for their needs. Therefore it seemed that homemade nuclear power on a large scale was the obvious answer to the needs of the new factories, swifter transport and improved public services that the Six hoped to provide.

By pooling their joint resources they planned to reduce the enormous cost of nuclear research and development. And they calculated, too, that working together they stood a better chance of catching up with the United States, the Soviet Union and Great Britain, the leading powers in the field of nuclear energy. The terms of Euratom laid down hard and fast regulations limiting the member countries to the development of nuclear power for peaceful purposes only.

Euratom was not the resounding success or unifying influence the ministers hoped for. At the time it was founded, France was the only nation of the Six with any appreciable nuclear industry. West Germany had very recently been permitted to embark on nuclear research, and the other four countries had hardly begun. It was not long before differences of opinion arose within Euratom. France was determined to build an independent nuclear military force, and de Gaulle objected to a form of cooperation which would compel him to place French nuclear power under "supranational," or European, control. At the same time, he refused to share nuclear knowledge or materials with the rest of the Six.

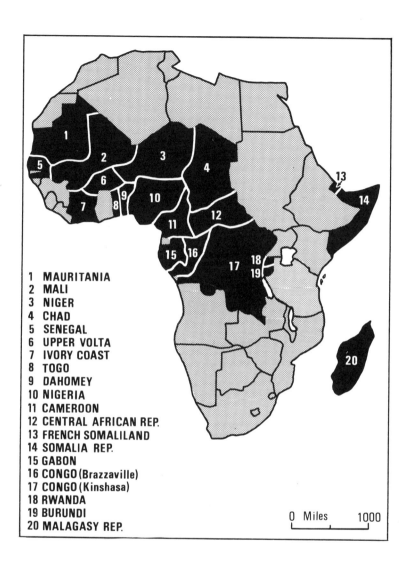

1 MAURITANIA
2 MALI
3 NIGER
4 CHAD
5 SENEGAL
6 UPPER VOLTA
7 IVORY COAST
8 TOGO
9 DAHOMEY
10 NIGERIA
11 CAMEROON
12 CENTRAL AFRICAN REP.
13 FRENCH SOMALILAND
14 SOMALIA REP.
15 GABON
16 CONGO (Brazzaville)
17 CONGO (Kinshasa)
18 RWANDA
19 BURUNDI
20 MALAGASY REP.

0   Miles   1000

Associated African Countries

Meanwhile the whole nuclear horizon widened. The United States Government poured millions of dollars into the nuclear industry. In a few years' time American firms made sensational advances and captured the nuclear markets of the Western world. The smaller nations could not compete, and Euratom was short of money and over-shadowed by American production. Although Euratom continues to play a useful part in training scientists, it has so far failed to establish a flourishing nuclear industry in Western Europe and, lacking French support, it has had a diminishing influence on the atomic policy of the Six.

9

THE GRASS ROOTS OF EUROPE

THE ORGANIZATION of agriculture presented even more intricate problems than that of industry, and the members of the Spaak Committee worked for a long time before they found a draft formula which took into account the needs of the farmers of all six countries, and was also acceptable to their governments. The farmers of the Six form a very powerful political group. In 1958 in Britain about four percent, and in the United States about six percent, of the population earned a living off the land. But in the Common Market countries the proportion was far higher. In Italy approximately thirty-three percent, in France twenty percent, and in West Germany twelve percent of all the working people were farmers. They were then, and still are, underpaid compared to the men and women employed in industry. When there is an election, they have a chance to express their discontent, and party leaders have to give careful consideration to the farmers' demands if they are going to win their votes.

The Spaak Committee called in agricultural experts

from all the member countries to carry out surveys, compile statistics, and suggest means of improving farming conditions. They were well aware of the human and economic difficulties ahead, for country people are often inclined to resist change. Frequently they prefer to carry on as their fathers and grandfathers have done before them, and it takes time and tact to persuade them that farming reforms are in their best interest.

One of the main troubles of Common Market farming lies in the smallness of many family holdings. The surveys showed that millions of farmers own less than twenty-five acres, and however hard they and their families work, they cannot make a decent living. In the ten years since the Common Market came into being, farming committees have encouraged small farmers to merge their tiny plots, share their equipment and gather their animals together for group management. But it was generally agreed that the farmers must act voluntarily and that no pressure should be brought to bear on the farming communities. All the governments could do was to offer rewards for group farming. At the same time they gave grants to a number of young farmers who, tempted by the opportunities of expanding industry, were moving to the towns and cities, leaving more land for those who remained in the country. This farm-to-factory migration has eased the situation, but has by no means solved it.

As part of their agricultural program, the member governments promoted schemes to modernize farms and

Gathering olives in the traditional way in Southern Italy

increase production per acre, or per animal, by the use of up-to-date equipment, efficient fertilizers and scientific feeding. Throughout the fields and vineyards, orchards and forests of the Common Market countries, bulldozers are grinding out new roads, horses are giving way to gleaming red tractors, electric milking machines are pumping away, and millions of tons of grapes and olives are being crushed by giant mechanical presses. A man can do more work in a day than he could in a week with antiquated tools.

In the last decade, thanks to enormous government expenditure, the farmers of the Six have greatly improved their yield. They have harvested bigger crops of corn, grown more fruit and vegetables, fattened up their sheep, cows and pigs to record weights, and hatched more chickens than ever before. Above all they have produced an immense quantity of milk, and turned it into cheese and butter.

Agricultural wages have risen according to plan, but the price of foodstuffs has gone up with them. The combination of massive production and high prices has created a crisis in the Community. Farmers are producing more food than they can sell, particularly butter. In the United States the price of one pound of butter is about 80 cents. In the markets of the Six, it ranges from a dollar in the Netherlands, to $1.20 in Italy, and it is a luxury that many housewives buy sparingly. Most country families get along very well without butter on their bread. They eat long crusty loaves by the yard, spaghetti, cheese, various kinds of sausage, vegetables, a limited amount of fish and meat, and always soup. In many districts large quantities of surplus butter remain unsold. It is estimated that in April 1969, the butter surplus reached 300,000 pounds. According to agreed agricultural policy, the governments buy up the butter, but when they get it they can only reduce it to cooking fat or sell it off at cut prices to undeveloped countries. Because of the large farming area and the richness of the land, production is higher in France than in the other five countries, and the glut of surplus food greater.

On December 10, 1968 Dr. Sicco Mansholt, agricultural expert and Vice-President of the Commission, made drastic proposals to reform Common Market farming on a ten-year plan. He reviewed the present situation and looked to the future. He explored ways and means of raising the standard of living of farming families, bringing their earnings into line with industrial wages, and providing nourishing food for the 187 million people of the Common Market countries at a price they could afford to pay. Mansholt restated his conviction that the main hope for the farmers, and for the government budgets, lies in merging the small farms so that families can earn a reasonable living. At the same time he based his plan on the prospect of absorbing farmers into the ever-expanding industry. He foresaw an increasing demand for manpower, and the farmers moving in to make up the numbers, so that at the end of the ten years there would be fewer farmers sharing the profits of the land. He urged the governments to set up retraining schemes, and reduce the crippling sums they were paying out on agriculture by helping the farmers to help themselves. In February 1969 the Mansholt Plan was presented to the Council of Ministers for consideration and approval.

The original aim of the economic experts was to

Sicco L. Mansholt

create a duty free trade in foodstuffs that would enable
farm produce passing from one Common Market country
to another to be priced at a common level. If this ideal
arrangement had worked out in practice, it would have
meant that corn and wine, bacon and eggs, milk, butter
and cheese, veal, beef and lamb and all the rest of the
farm produce would be bought and sold for the same
prices in shops and markets throughout the Six. House-
wives would have such a wide variety of food to choose
from that they would insist on high quality, and the
standard would be maintained by the natural laws of supply and demand. Under these ideal conditions the Common Market agriculturalists hoped to set prices at a reasonable level which would both satisfy the shoppers and
provide the farmers with a decent living. The target date
for common pricing was set at July, 1968.

But the policy of common pricing broke down under
pressure of economic events. It was already a controversial
issue when, in August 1969, the French Government devalued the franc by thirteen percent. French finances had
been unstable for some time, and by the devaluation
President Pompidou, who had recently succeeded General
de Gaulle, hoped to put them in order and restore confidence in the value of the franc in other countries.

Once the franc became cheaper, the rate of exchange
became more favorable to overseas customers, and the
government saw that if French manufacturers and mer-

chants could sell more goods to foreign buyers, the proceeds would stimulate industry at home and strengthen the French economy.

The French farmers immediately arose in violent protest against the imposition of a set price on their produce according to Common Market principles. They pointed out that if they were compelled to sell at a price fixed before the devaluation, they would be losing thirteen percent of their profits and could not possibly support their families.

At a marathon meeting of the agricultural experts of the Six on August 13, it was agreed to exempt France from the rules of the common agricultural policy for two years to allow the farmers to adapt their organization to the new rate of exchange.

Two months later, in October 1969, the Germans struck another blow at the Common Market agricultural financial policy by upgrading the value of the mark by 9.29 percent. Although it created complications for agriculture, the revaluation of the mark was beneficial for the European Economic Community as a whole. German industry had become so strong and so efficient since the foundation of the Federal Republic in 1949, that the other five Common Market countries were finding it more and more difficult to compete. The situation was in direct contrast to that in France because once the mark is more valuable, German goods are more expensive if they are paid for in foreign currencies. Therefore prospective buyers are likely to explore other markets, and possibly buy less from Germany and more from the other five Common Market countries.

Germany industry was strong enough to stand the strain, but German agriculture, like the French, faced a crisis. If the prices of farm produce rose with the mark, people both inside and outside West Germany would have had to pay more for their food. Consequently they would buy less and the surpluses would mount.

After long and heated discussion the Common Market ministers of finance and agriculture agreed to make a second exception to the common pricing policy. They conceded that German farmers should be subsidized in order to keep their prices down. They would sell their produce at the prices quoted before revaluation, and the German Government would compensate them for four years for their loss of income in not keeping up the mark. The total cost of this farm subsidy was calculated at $464,500,000, and it was agreed that the Community farm fund, which was made up of contributions from the member nations, would pay 12.5 percent of the total cost.

This was a momentous decision, for it was contrary to the principles of the Treaty of Rome. But it was a definite sign that the leading figures in Common Market affairs had accepted the fact that the original terms of the agricultural policy had been too rigid. Many serious supporters of the Common Market are hopeful that with this new flexibility many of the outstanding problems can be solved without destroying the basic structure of agricultural integration.

10

MANAGING THE EUROPEAN COMMUNITY

Today the European Community, still generally known as the Common Market, is a huge, active, fast-growing and exciting adventure. It takes care of 187 million people living in an area of 449,000 square miles. Seventy-five million of them work at various trades, arts and professions. They manufacture fine merchandise and they cultivate large areas of land. As a result, the European Community is the world's largest trader. It even surpasses the United States in its volume of imports and exports. The success of an international institution of such immense size and scope depends largely on efficient, conscientious and imaginative administration. The men at the top have to be exceptional; and all the way down the payroll the Community staff have great responsibilities. They are under international scrutiny and a bad calculation can ruin the economy, and careless conduct can tarnish the image, of European unity.

In 1958 there were in Western Europe three distinct communities: the Coal and Steel Community, the Economic Community, and the Atomic Energy Community. But even though they were constituted by separate treaties, their spheres of interest were closely related, and their work fitted together like the pieces of a jigsaw puzzle.

There was good reason for this joint buildup of Community thought and action. Many of the same men were concerned in drawing up the three treaties, and they intended them to be a blueprint for political unity and the basis of eventual federal government. Almost all the statesmen and other officials who are striving to preserve the principles of the treaties, and carrying out the day-to-day and month-to-month work of the Communities recognize the importance of this long-term program and they support it wholeheartedly.

The membership of the three Communities is identical and it has not changed since the Treaty of Paris was signed by Belgium, France, West Germany, Italy, Luxembourg and the Netherlands. When the headquarters of the Coal and Steel Community were established in Luxembourg, they attracted business and wealth to the little landbound duchy. Luxembourg covers an area of a thousand square miles, a dot on the map of Europe when compared to France with 212,895 square miles. A hereditary sovereign, the Grand Duke Jean, rules over a population of 330,000 which was suddenly swelled by its Coal and Steel connections. Statesmen and permanent officials with their staffs came to administer the Community. Soon business executives, lawyers and bankers arrived to confer and negotiate. There were always members of the press waiting to report on the meetings, photograph the celebrities, and write up the recurring crises.

Since 1919 Luxembourg has had close links with Belgium; and in 1948 the government signed the Brussels Treaty with Belgium and the Netherlands, creating Benelux—a three-power customs union and a forerunner of European cooperation. For these countries, therefore, the Coal and Steel Community, the Common Market and the Atomic Energy Community were a vast new application of their belief in economic union.

The ultimate aims of economic and political union are presented in the Treaty of Paris and in the two Treaties of Rome in slightly different words, but they all add up to the same objective. Because the work of each Community dovetails into the others, it seemed from the beginning sensible and almost inevitable that in time they would forge closer links and merge into one European community.

They were originally directed by three separate decision-making bodies—the Councils of Ministers—and run by three executive bodies. The founders of the Coal and Steel Community decided to name their executive body a High Authority, while the Economic Community and Euratom called the official groups who did this same kind of work Commissions. All three Communities worked with a single European Parliament and a European Court of Justice. An Economic and Social Committee served the

Common Market and Euratom in an advisory capacity; and the Coal and Steel Community sought advice from a consultative Committee, and raised money for its considerable running-expenses by taxing the turnover of the firms subject to the High Authority. The Common Market and Euratom budgets were contributed by the member governments at a fixed rate according to their national means: France, Germany and Italy 28 percent, Belgium and the Netherlands, 7.9 percent and Luxembourg 0.2 percent.

These contributions were based on the parity, or the exchange value, of the various currencies compared to the United States dollar. After the French devaluation and the German revaluation the same parities ceased to exist because a dollar would buy more francs and fewer marks than before. Therefore it would cost France more, and Germany less, to fulfill their financial obligations to the Community, and this is obviously unfair. It was clear that a fresh scale of contributions would have to be worked out, or a whole new financial system introduced.

Since July 1967 all three Communities have been administered by a single executive Commission, situated in Brussels, which replaced the European Coal and Steel Community High Authority and the Common Market and Euratom Commissions. At the same time the decision-making bodies were merged in a single Council of Ministers, also in Brussels. The Court of Justice, serving the

The Institutions of the European Communities

EXECUTIVE ACTION

Council of Ministers

European Commission

Consultative Committee

Economic and Social Committee

JUDICIAL CONTROL
Court of Justice

DEMOCRATIC CONTROL
European Parliament

Community as a whole, sits in Luxembourg. The European Parliament, also representing the entire Community, has an impressive secretariat building in Luxembourg, and borrows the premises of the Council of Europe at Strasbourg for a session lasting about a week from eight to ten times a year.

The merger of the three Communities, embracing all the activities of the Six, was generally regarded as an important move in the direction of European unity. The first President, Jean Rey, an eminent Belgian lawyer and politician, is greatly respected throughout the Community. The new European Commission building is an expression of faith and an architectural adventure. It is laid out in the shape of an X, and it was the first edifice in Europe to be constructed on a new American system, radiating from a central core with surrounding walls suspended on steel arms.

The Council of Ministers is composed of six ministers who hold high political posts in the governments of their own countries. They may be the Foreign Ministers, but Ministers of Trade, Transport, Housing, Education, Agriculture and other government departments also attend Council meetings to give expert advice on their own subjects. These members of the Council of Ministers are official representatives of their governments, and their job is to protect the national interests of their own countries, and at the same time to further European integration. At present they are considering a three-year plan, presented to them by the Commission, for removing the remaining barriers to free trade; modernizing industry, coordinating rail, road and inland water transport and deciding just what the governments of the Six can demand in return for the subsidies they hand out. The Council of Ministers is also considering proposals for doctors, dentists, pharmacists and pharmaceutical firms to practice or carry on business throughout the Community. Similar exchange proposals extend to architects and journalists, and they are all under discussion. These members of the Council of Ministers are appointed by the Prime Ministers of their own countries to carry out the work.

Council motions are decided by weighted voting. This means that the Six have voting power according to their size and political importance: France, Germany and Italy have four votes each, Belgium and the Netherlands two, and Luxembourg one. Out of this total of seventeen, twelve votes constitute a majority and approve a proposal. On a proposal that is presented by the Commission, any twelve votes must be cast by at least four countries out of the Six. This prevents the three small countries from being overruled if the three big ones gang up against them. Every member country, and at least eighty other countries, send ambassadors to Brussels accredited to the headquarters of the European Community. They have official residences, permanent staffs and diplomatic privileges in the same manner as ambassadors in capitals all over the world.

The Councils of Ministers make the final decisions, but the groundwork and the actual organization is carried out by the fourteen members of the Commission and their staffs. The function of the Commission, and its approach to the organization of the Community, are very different from those of the Council. The members of the Commission are not official representatives of their particular countries, appointed to carry out government instructions. On the contrary, they are free to express their own views, committed to uphold the principles of the founding treaties, and pledged to act in the interest of the Community as a whole. At least twenty-eight men, experienced in foreign affairs, are presented to the Council by the governments of the Six as prospective candidates for seats on the Commission. The fourteen members finally selected serve a term of four years. They prepare proposals for approval by the Council, and when the ministers have taken a decision they put it into practice. The Commission and the Council hold their meetings in secret and their sessions are not reported. The sessions of the European Parliament and the Court of Justice are held in public, open to the press or anyone else who cares to attend.

The members of the Commission work fulltime all year, assisted by a large secretariat staffed by specialists in the areas covered by the Community as a whole. They include economists, engineers, farmers, teachers, scientists, writers, translators, secretaries and all the other personnel needed to operate a big international organization. They

A language lab in the European School in Brussels

all speak several languages and some are fluent in four or five.

Many children of Community families are educated at one of the six "European" schools which are financed by Community funds. The students work in two languages and learn to look at life from an international point of view because all the subjects, and especially history and geography, are taught from a European, and never from a national, angle. Children from the Community schools graduate with a European diploma which is recognized by all the universities of the Six member countries, and also by Austria.

The Treaty of Paris provided for a parliamentary assembly to exercise democratic control over the actions of the High Authority. When the Common Market and Euratom were set up, the assembly was enlarged from seventy-eight to one hundred forty-two members, and its powers extended to the Common Market and Euratom. It then became known as the European Parliament. It is not a parliament in the ordinary meaning of the word, with the power to make laws and enforce them. Its duties are to supervise the work of the Commission, to scrutinize its annual reports and to provide—in the periodic sessions at Strasbourg, and through written and oral questions— regular opportunities for consultation and debate on mat- ters of Community interest. At present the European Parliament has the right to inspect the Community budgets and examine the way they are spent, and there is talk of granting it far greater financial powers. Of one hundred and forty-two members: thirty-six each come from France, Germany and Italy; fourteen each from Belgium and the Netherlands; and six from Luxembourg. They elect a president and other parliamentary officials from among their own members.

It is an interesting development of the European Parliament that the members sit as political groups, not

A meeting of the European Parliament

as national delegations. They have chosen this seating plan of their own accord and it has become an accepted custom. The political parties represented in the European Parliament are mainly Christian Democrats, Liberals and Socialists, with a small representation of Communists and French Gaullist supporters. They are all members of parliament in their respective countries and are appointed by their governments in proportion to the strength of the political parties at home. In order to give the European Parliament greater standing and authority, it has been suggested that eventually, when general elections are held in the various countries, there should be two sets of candidates—one set for a national parliament and the other for the European Parliament at Strasbourg. The proposal has won active support, and it is under review.

The European Court of Justice, situated in Luxembourg, is the court of final appeal for the Community. It is a court of appeal available to the Commission if it considers that some member state has failed to fulfill its Treaty obligations. The Court is also open to groups of people, firms or private individuals, if they wish to bring actions against the Council or the Committee for injustice, loss or damage caused by the application of the terms of the Treaty. The Court of Justice is the only body sufficiently powerful to decide on the rights and wrongs of an act by the Council of Ministers or by the Commission.

The Court consists of seven judges, at least one from every member country, appointed by the governments of

Judges of the European Court consider a case

the member states. The judges are all eminent men of high legal standing in their own countries, and their decisions carry great weight. At present, Community law is concerned solely with the interpretation and application of the terms of the three Treaties. It applies the established legal code, acceptable to the Six, to the settlement of their disputes, and to bringing them into line if they infringe any of the Treaty rules. By 1969 the Court had considered well over five-hundred cases, and though it has been in existence only fourteen years, it has so much prestige that no member government has ever opposed its pronouncements or failed to carry out its rulings.

On the fringes of Community administration there are two committees which exert considerable influence on the shaping of Community policies. The Economic and Social Committee serves the Common Market and Euratom, and the Consultative Committee does the same for the Coal and Steel Community. The Economic and Social Committee is composed of a hundred-and-one members, and they are chosen by Trade Union officials and the leading men of many professions to represent a wide variety of economic and social activity. Doctors, professors, factory workers, farmers, salesmen, carpenters, plumbers, artists, writers and any other responsible citizens are eligible to sit on the Economic and Social Committee. The Consultative Committee is composed of fifty-one members: trade unionists, employers from the coal and steel industry, and their customers.

Each country is expected to select for membership in the two Committees a cross section of its own people to voice public opinion. The Council nominates successful candidates for four years. At present the Consultative Committee which serves the Coal and Steel Community is made up of employers, workers—many of whom are trade unionists—and a "general interest" group. At first the workers were antagonistic to the employers, and very suspicious indeed of the third group who they regarded as intellectuals and spies for the employers.

But the system of the two committees has worked remarkably well. There have been political, religious and social differences, but none of the groups have worked on a national basis. As they do not have authority to act on their own initiative, they can only weigh different points of view and wait until they are consulted. The Council of Ministers and the central Committee do not have to accept their advice, but they are wise to take it into account. The hundred and fifty-two members of the two committees are enthusiastic members of the Six, and they frequently have an impact on community opinion.

11

CHANGE OF MIND IN BRITAIN

WHEN THE LEADERS of the Community countries invited
Britain to join the coal and steel merger and, four years
later, to take part in the discussions at Messina, most of
them were genuinely anxious to gradually eliminate trade
barriers and build a united Europe in partnership with
the British Government. Viewing the evident success of
the Marshall Plan, and the absolute necessity of building
a strong Europe as a defense against Communist expansion, British membership in the Community seemed to
them a natural stage in the sequence of events. As General de Gaulle was out of office and no other European
leader was openly opposed to partnership with Britain,
it seems that in 1957 there would have been comparatively
little difficulty in expanding the Community of Six into
a Community of Seven, or more.

But the invitation to Messina was the last approach
the Six ever made to Britain. When they had been
turned down twice they were not prepared to be snubbed
again. They decided to press on with their own plans
and leave England out of their calculations.

At this point British statesmen were not at all worried. They had no doubt of their wisdom in upholding their independence and keeping clear of Common Market entanglements. They relied on the traditional trade with the Commonwealth countries to provide ample markets for British goods, and to keep up the standard of living to which the country was accustomed. At the same time the British Government intended to maintain, and increase, trade with the United States and Europe, but only on its own terms.

Trade between Britain and the member countries of the Commonwealth has for some time past been regulated by a system known as "imperial preference." This entails a special arrangement of buying and selling within the Commonwealth which proved very successful until the whole balance of world trade was upset by the Second World War.

Imperial preference was based on a system which enabled Commonwealth countries, such as Australia, Canada, New Zealand, and India, to ship their large stocks of surplus food and raw materials to Britain and take in exchange the manufactured goods which they did not have the factories to produce at home. For instance, Australia sold mainly wool, wheat and mineral ores; Canada grain, minerals and timber; and New Zealand wool, mutton and lamb and dairy products such as butter, eggs and cheese. India exported rice, sugar, silks and spices. In return they all imported machinery, vehicles, tools, clothes, medical supplies and innumerable other machinemade British goods.

The system of imperial preference also controlled customs duties and kept them at a lower rate for imports from one British dominion to another than for goods imported from the rest of the world. Thus the Australians paid less duty on a British car than on an American one, and British buyers paid less for New Zealand butter than for butter from Denmark. This preferential treatment gave Commonwealth goods an advantage, for shopkeepers could sell them more cheaply than foreign goods since they did not carry such a high duty. As part of the bargain, Britain and the other members of the Commonwealth also agreed to abide by the imperial tariff rate and promised not to make individual deals or to reduce the duty on foreign goods coming into their countries in order to tempt new customers and open up fresh markets.

This system of imperial trade worked smoothly until the Second World War. Britain held a powerful position in the world and British goods were renowned for their quality. The Commonwealth countries were proud of their special relationship with the Crown, and grateful for the protection against outside trade competition. But gradually their situation has changed. The Commonwealth governments have encouraged immigration from Western and Eastern Europe, and they have extended a special welcome to applicants with technical skill and business experience. New industries have grown up and

A Commonwealth Conference

the manufacturers are anxious to sell their own products, instead of giving way to British goods. Australia and New Zealand have increased their trade with Europe and have built up a thriving business connection with Japan. They want to be free to make their own commercial agreements without being hampered by imperial restrictions.

During and after the war the bombed factories in Britain could hardly produce enough goods to meet the basic needs at home, let alone ship them across the Atlantic. So Canada turned more and more toward the United States, until Canadian farmers and manufacturers are now buying and selling more in American markets than they are in British.

British politicians were slow to accept the changing scene. They had clung to the established pattern of Commonwealth preference for two main reasons. First, because it seemed to present a safe and ever-expanding market for British goods; and second, because they had inherited a deep-seated sense of responsibility for the welfare of the Commonwealth countries and they had a real fear of letting them down.

When Mr. Bretherton returned from Messina, he reported on the high intellectual standard of the discussions. It was evident that many of the most brilliant men in Europe, both politicians and economists, considered the planning of the European Economic Community a top priority project. But the British Prime Minister, Anthony Eden, and Harold Macmillan, the Chancellor of the Exchequer, were not sufficiently impressed to try to join the group.

Gradually, however, directors of British firms saw that European markets were closing against them, and certain politicians sensed that the policy of splendid isolation was leaving Britain out in the cold. In 1957 there was a financial slump which caused general disquiet, and a growing number of industrialists began to suspect that somewhere there was something radically wrong with the pattern of British trade.

In January of 1957, Anthony Eden resigned. He was succeeded as Prime Minister by Harold Macmillan who had shared Eden's views on the value of a separate Britain. But the government was faced by strikes and mounting discontent. It was clear that something must be done. While the Spaak committee was busy in Brussels drafting the Treaty of Rome, Macmillan put forward a proposal for a large free trade area to be formed by all the eighteen member countries of the Organization for European Economic Cooperation. The plan was clearly designed to protect British interests and maintain the links with the Commonwealth. It concentrated on industry, and touched very fleetingly on agriculture. The main difference between the Macmillan plan and that of the Common Market lay in the provisions for foreign trade. By the terms of the Treaty of Rome the Six agreed to charge a common rate of duty on imports from the rest of the world; but by the terms of the British plan, nations would be free to fix their own rate of duty on overseas imports. To the British Government this seemed a reasonable arrangement which would enable the country to form closer ties with Europe without abandoning the Commonwealth. But the Six suspected that Britain was trying to get the best of both worlds. They immediately asked to postpone discussion of a large free trade area so that the Spaak committee could complete its work without any interruption.

Later the same year the Common Market came into action, and the results rapidly exceeded the expectations of its most ardent supporters. Within the Six, production leaped ahead and trade increased enormously. British pessimists who had predicted the failure of the whole venture were cautious. They watched the trade figures and anxiously compared their own to those of the Six.

In 1959 Great Britain got together with Denmark, Norway, Sweden and Switzerland to discuss their common problems. The Scandinavian countries had close trade links with Britain, and had therefore adopted the British attitude to the Schuman Plan and the European Economic Community. Switzerland had preserved its traditional neutrality and detachment and had also taken no part in the deliberations of the Six. From the 1959 meeting the European Free Trade Association, commonly known as EFTA, was born. The five countries invited Austria to join them, and soon afterwards Portugal invited

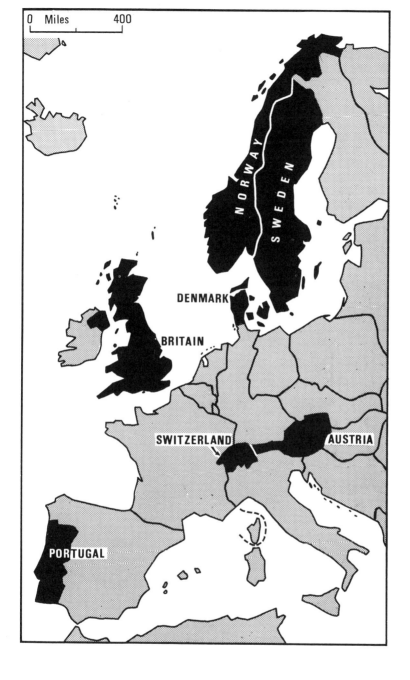

0 Miles 400

NORWAY

SWEDEN

DENMARK

BRITAIN

SWITZERLAND

AUSTRIA

PORTUGAL

European Free Trade Countries

itself. This was an unexpected complication and an embarrassment because Portugal was an undemocratic police state ruled by a dictator, President Antonio de Oliveria Salazar, and the other countries did not approve of the regime. However they finally decided to accept the Portuguese application, and in November 1959 they signed the EFTA convention. In 1961 Finland joined EFTA as an associate member. From this time onwards Western Europe was split in two between the Common Market Six, working toward full integration, and the EFTA Seven, concerned only with reducing tariffs in industrial affairs with a very slight emphasis on agriculture, and none on future political union. The newspapers of the world reported with a touch of scorn that European politics were at Sixes and Sevens.

The real drive to launch EFTA came from the British, who by this time were very anxious to bridge the gap between the Six and the rest of Western Europe. Other EFTA countries were eager to gain either full membership or association with the Common Market, but they agreed that Britain should take the lead.

In August 1961 Harold Macmillan officially reversed his former policy and sent off a formal letter of application for full membership in the Common Market. In the same month Ireland and Denmark also requested entry, soon after followed by Norway.

In November 1961 the negotiations between Britain

and the Common Market countries opened in Brussels, and the other applicants awaited the outcome of the discussions and prepared to negotiate for themselves if Britain was successful.

12

THE GENERAL TAKES OVER

France

F<small>ROM THE MOMENT</small> he returned to power on June 1, 1958,
General de Gaulle was a dominant figure in the affairs of
Western Europe. He is a controversial character and
many of his decisions are difficult to understand. It may be
helpful to go back briefly to the summer of 1944, when the
Free French fighting-forces advanced side by side with the
British and American Armies from the beaches of Nor-
mandy to the outskirts of Paris.

The Western Allies readily agreed that the French
should have the honor of liberating their own capital.
Within the city French patriots rose against the Nazi
garrison, and from without an armored column broke
through the defenses and accepted the surrender of the
Nazi commander. On August 26, General de Gaulle and
General Leclerc, who had commanded the Free French
Army in battle, marched at the head of triumphant
troops from the Arc de Triomphe—where the flame of
the unknown warrior who was killed in the First World
War burned once more—down the broad boulevard of

the Champs Elysées to the cathedral of Notre Dame, for a service of joyous thanksgiving. The men and women of the French resistance, who had fought the underground war and risked everything for this day, emerged from four years of hiding. The route was lined with patriotic crowds acclaiming de Gaulle as a savior and leader, for everyone knew that, more than any other man, it was he who had kept the spirit of France alive through the dark days of defeat until the dawn of victory.

But French troubles were by no means ended. The night after the parade, German bombers inflicted a heavy raid on Paris, killing a thousand people and wounding thousands more. Throughout the country transport was almost at a standstill, and although many outlying farms and villages had plenty of food, the inhabitants of the big city were almost starving because there was no way of delivering it to them.

Two weeks after the liberation General de Gaulle became head of a provisional government, and started to tackle some of the most pressing problems. The political situation was highly inflammable because of the intense antagonism between the French who had resisted the Nazis, and those who had collaborated with them. Foremost among the resisters were the French Communists. They had become very influential and de Gaulle was compelled to include them in his government as a reward for their services, and also because they would make trouble if they were left out. In the early postwar period, the two other main political parties in France were the Socialists and the M.R.P. (Mouvement Républicain Populaire), a progressive Catholic Party. All three parties were represented in the provisional government.

At the time of the liberation Marshal Pétain was in Switzerland where he would certainly have been permitted to remain, for few Frenchmen wanted to take revenge on the old man for his part in the surrender of 1940. But, at the age of eighty-nine, Pétain insisted on returning to France to stand trial. The court condemned him to death for treason, but de Gaulle succeeded in changing the sentence to life imprisonment. Pierre Laval, however, was also sentenced to death and swiftly executed.

In November 1945 the French people voted for a Constituent Assembly, the members of which unanimously elected de Gaulle to lead them. It was an uneasy task; France was heading for an acute financial crisis and the only way out was through American aid. East–West relations were worsening rapidly and de Gaulle saw that the United States Government would never be prepared to put money into a country where Communists held any political power. Sandwiched between Communism, which he detested, and United States support, which he resented, de Gaulle found himself in an impossible situation. In January 1946 he suddenly decided to resign and let some other leader tackle the awkward setup. He was then fifty-six years old, and resolved ultimately to guide the destiny of France. His departure from the Élysée Palace was accompanied by a chorus of admiration and regret; and he can have had no idea that he was taking a step which would keep him out of office for the next twelve years.

After his resignation de Gaulle built up, under his own personal leadership, a new political mass movement which bore the stirring title of the Rally of the French People (Rassemblement du Peuple Français), or R.P.F. It operated with carefully prepared publicity and military precision. It has been said that the R.P.F. was the worst mistake de Gaulle ever made. At first it seemed to be a success, and many voters were attracted by the glamor of the new party. But the French are an independent, hard-headed and down-to-earth people. They soon began to compare the antics of the R.P.F. to the trappings of Nazism, and they distrusted the arrogance and totalitar-ian attitude of de Gaulle. In 1951, when the nation voted for a moderate, reformed Constitution and proclaimed a Fourth Republic, the R.P.F. won only 117 votes out of a total of 627. De Gaulle was forced out, against his will, into a political wilderness.

The 1950's were stormy years for France. French armies fought and lost the war in Indochina, food at home was scarce and the black market rampant. Moreover, no one political party was strong enough to form a lasting government. But as the Berlin blockade and the Soviet occupation of Eastern Europe turned public opinion against Communism, the Americans began to strengthen the French economy with Marshall Aid. Though governments rose and fell in rapid succession, conditions gradually improved, and the French people began to look beyond their own frontiers. The idea of a united Western Europe took firm root and prospered.

Before the war de Gaulle had bought an old posting inn at Colombey-les-Deux Églises, in the country northeast of Paris. It was a lovely house in a wild woodland setting and he had spent many happy family holidays there. After his political defeat, de Gaulle left Paris with his wife and settled down at Colombey-les-Deux-Églises to meditate and write his *Mémoires*. Madame de Gaulle was a serene, housewifely woman, a devoted wife and mother. She and her husband had had one family tragedy, for after two perfectly normal children, first a boy and then a girl, they had a daughter who was mentally deficient and blind. They were absolutely devoted to Anne, this mongoloid child, and Madame de Gaulle hardly ever left her. They were so anxious for Anne's future after their death that de Gaulle founded a home for young girls with incurable diseases, and endowed it handsomely with the proceeds of the first volume of his *Mémoires*. If Anne had lived, she would have been well cared for by the sisters of a Catholic order. But she died very suddenly of pneumonia at the age of twenty. A close friend of the family related that when Madame de Gaulle

Colombey-les-deux-Églises, the country home of Charles de Gaulle

broke down at the funeral, her husband comforted her by saying: "Why do you weep? Now Anne is like every other young girl."

Although Madame de Gaulle took no outward part in politics, her ardent Catholicism and her unshakable sense of duty had a profound effect on the people around her. Men who had been divorced, or fell short of her high moral standards, were not invited to the de Gaulle luncheons, dinners or receptions, and they seldom attained high office.

In daily life Madame de Gaulle's placidity was almost indestructible. After the General's retirement she flew around the world with him on a tour of the French possessions, in an aircraft presented to him by President Truman. Hour after hour she sat in a separate seat, knitting incessantly from continent to continent, and joining him only at mealtimes. As the General gave orders to touch down on foreign territory only in the most exceptional circumstances, and the distances between some of the French airfields were very great indeed, fuel ran dangerously low on several occasions. But Madame de Gaulle's needles flicked on and she appeared unmoved.

During his retreat at Colombey, the General brooded on the decline of French grandeur, deplored the dependence on American bounty, condemned the idea of the European Army, and criticized every other move to integrate France into a Western European Community. He made periodic trips to Paris, and received a few select politicians and foreign diplomats at Colombey. He entertained Konrad Adenauer as a guest of the family, be-

Charles de Gaulle

cause he knew that they both genuinely believed in
Franco-German friendship. De Gaulle had moments of
abysmal depression. After the liberation he had jubilantly
proclaimed: "I am France." At Colombey he was heard
to say: "I was France." But he never really gave up the

idea of France leading Europe, and de Gaulle leading France. The R.P.F. died a natural death, and he made no move to save it.

In 1958 de Gaulle got his big chance and he seized it without hesitation. There is no doubt that his restoration was the result of most careful and shrewd political planning. The crisis which wrecked the Fourth Republic arose through the revolt against French rule by the Arab population of the North African colony of Algeria. A million French Christian settlers had moved to Algeria and made good there. They had worked hard, and many had established a better standard of living than they had ever enjoyed in France. But they lived side by side with Algerian-born Muslim Arabs who were desperately poor and increasingly resentful. These native Algerians could not learn to read and write because the French Government provided so few schools, and they were barred from good jobs because they had no education or training. They had real grounds for complaint, and on October 31, 1954 they staged an armed rebellion which developed into outright war between France and Algeria.

Units of the French Army were dispatched to Algeria to restore order. But, it was not a matter to be settled solely by military means. There was right and wrong on both sides, and after four years of growing bitterness and bloodshed, there was still no just solution in sight.

Although he was now a background figure, de Gaulle remained to many Frenchmen a symbol of success. He seemed to be the only man who could command respect in both France and Algeria, and the loyalty of the officers and troops who were heartily sick of the struggle.

De Gaulle was ready for the challenge. On June 1, 1958 he answered the call, and accepted the post of Premier of the ailing Fourth Republic. He disclaimed allegiance to any particular party, and declared in glowing phrases his sole purpose—to ensure the solidarity and the prosperity of France. The words of de Gaulle had a real impact; an immense wave of relief swept through the country at the prospect of firm leadership.

Almost immediately after he took office de Gaulle began to work on a new Constitution more in keeping with his ideas of modern conditions than the one his successors had drafted in 1947. In December 1958, by an overwhelming majority, de Gaulle was elected President of the Fifth Republic of France.

In Algeria things went from bad to worse. The French settlers clung desperately to their rights, their homes and their livelihood, and the Arabs were resolved to drive them out. Both Christians and Muslims committed savage acts of terrorism against each other. Although in 1958 de Gaulle declared that he was in favor of an agreement whereby Algeria would remain under French rule, he probably realized that it would never work. Three years later he fixed a date for referendums in France and Algeria, so that the people of both countries could vote for or against Algerian independence. Both referendums favored self-rule for Algeria. As a result of de Gaulle's policy, on July 3, 1962 Algeria became an independent republic. The French settlers felt abandoned and betrayed, and they lost faith in the French Government. But eventually three-quarters of a million French-Algerians returned to France, and, partly owing to the opportunities opened up by the Common Market, were able to make new lives there.

A month after the Algerian settlement, a political extremist on the side of the French settlers fired a volley of shots into de Gaulle's car as he and his wife drove to the airport on their way back to Colombey. The bullets missed the General by a bare inch, but neither he nor Madame de Gaulle showed the slightest sign of emotion.

The assassination attempt brought home to the French people what the loss of de Gaulle would mean. They had no substitute and no heir to take over from him. His popularity and prestige rose higher than ever before. Secure in the knowledge of his political strength, he turned his attention to European conditions in general, and the Common Market in particular.

13

BRITAIN WOOS THE SIX

WHILE FRANCE was struggling to find a way out of the tormented tangle of the Algerian war, Britain was trying to find a way into the Common Market.

Edward Heath, who held the post of Lord Privy Seal in Harold Macmillan's Conservative Government, was appointed negotiator-in-chief with the Six. The post of Lord Privy Seal is one which bears great prestige, but leaves the occupant free to carry out special missions for the government. In the summer of 1961 Heath was charged with the responsibility of protecting British interests, but at the same time getting Britain into the European Community. Behind him a team of experienced politicians and civil servants studied the pros and cons of British entry, ready to give advice on the many different aspects of the case. Everyone concerned realized that the negotiations would be complicated. But, having switched its policy and charted a new course to prosperity, the British Government was fairly optimistic about the outcome. Ministers knew that most of the Community was friendly to Britain, so they were not too worried about European reaction to their application. Their main anxiety was still the future of the Commonwealth.

At first the negotiators pictured a round-table conference, with delegates from the Six and from Britain presenting their proposals for general discussion. However, the Six decided that they would prefer to consider the various problems in private, while the British waited outside to receive their joint decisions. During the proceedings the Common Market Commission, under the efficient and impartial chairmanship of Professor Hallstein, acted as an advisory board for the Community as a whole. It was a clumsy process and very time-consuming; and it demanded infinite patience on the part of the members of the British team who spent hours hanging about in anterooms while the Six were making up their minds.

All through the summer of 1961 the British prepared their proposals for the first meeting which took place in Paris in October. The following meetings were held in Brussels in the Belgian Foreign Office, and continued all through the winter, the following spring, and on into the summer. The British were in an extremely delicate position. Since they were doing the asking, it was absolutely essential to show that they were ready to meet the demands of the Six at least halfway. But whenever they gave in to Community pressure, some Commonwealth country protested. There was no escaping the fact that Common-

wealth preference was in direct contradiction to the actual
terms of the Treaty of Rome and the spirit of European
unity. It was clear that if Britain got into the Common
Market, the government would have to terminate the
special concessions to the Commonwealth, and agree on a
common policy for external trade in much the same way
that the Six had formed an association with the African
territories.

Another formidable hurdle was the difference between the British and the Community agricultural policies. The British system provides the farmers with a
certain market for his goods at a guaranteed price. The
government pays a cash subsidy to the farmers to make
up the difference between the high cost of producing
milk, bacon, butter, eggs and other foodstuffs, and the
lower, official price at which they are allowed to sell them
in the market. It means, therefore, that the taxpayer
bears the cost of keeping the farmers in business, but
reaps the reward of buying food at a reasonable price.

At this time the Common Market countries' farm
prices were regulated by another system. Instead of being
pegged down to an artificially low level, they were controlled to a large extent by the cost of production. In
general they were, and still are, higher than British prices
so the consumer pays the actual cost of raising the crops
and rearing the animals. There is less security for the
farmers because if prices are very high, people do not buy
their produce; and also if farms grow too much fruit,

vegetables or grain, or make too much butter, there is a glut in the market and they cannot sell their produce at all—unless the government steps in and buys it up.

Agriculture has been one of the greatest problems the Common Market administrators have had to face. It has been much more difficult to handle agriculture than industry, and they were determined not to have the situation further complicated by the introduction of the British method, which was very different from their own. Later events narrowed the gap between the systems of British and Common Market farming, but in 1962, at the Brussels meeting, they seemed to be worlds apart.

The circumstances in Britain were different too. The Common Market countries produce nine-tenths of all the food they need, while Britain produces only half. Therefore it does not cost the British Government any more to pay subsidies to farmers than to buy extra food abroad at high prices. But as the British system did not fit in with Common Market agriculture, everyone realized that it would have to go; although the government saw that the public was going to object to rising prices, and the farmers would certainly protest at their loss of security. So the delegates at Brussels received instructions to get the best terms they could, and the negotiations dragged on while they tried to find a way of softening the blow.

The chief French delegate at the Common Market talks was Couve de Murville, a distinguished diplomat who was at that time Foreign Minister, and in 1968 be-

Harvesting grain by modern equipment in the Common Market

came Premier of France. Working closely with President de Gaulle, he upheld French interests in a manner which was courteous and studiously correct, though somewhat cold.

De Gaulle had other problems on his mind besides the British bid for the Common Market. Foremost among them was the question of nuclear arms. He was embittered by the fact that the United States Government was determined to keep control of the nuclear striking power of the Atlantic Alliance, and refused to share its nuclear knowledge with any nation except Britain, and this only because the two nations had worked together on the first Atomic bomb during the Second World War. In 1959, as a protest against American nuclear policy, de Gaulle withdrew the French Mediterranean fleet from NATO command and banned American nuclear warheads from French territory.

In the following year French scientists triumphantly exploded their first atomic bomb in the Sahara Desert, and France became—with the United States, the Soviet Union and Britain—the fourth atomic power in the world. But even after they had succeeded in splitting the atom, there remained a great deal of expensive and laborious research before the French could compete in nuclear armaments. In spite of the cost de Gaulle pressed on, for he was not satisfied with the American promise to defend Europe by nuclear means if the need arose. He wanted to equip the French Army with nuclear weapons, and reestablish France as a great military power, with a national nuclear deterrent subject to his own command, entirely independent of the United States.

Although the lack of a nuclear striking force and the thought of Anglo-American cooperation rankled, during the first year of the Common Market negotiations de Gaulle was tolerably friendly to Britain, cordial to Macmillan when they met, and outwardly prepared to accept British entry—always provided they could come to terms which did not conflict with French interests, or diminish French power.

Men like Jean Monnet, on the fringe of the negotiations, urged the British to get in first and thrash out the details later. But they dared not take a chance on it. They were prepared to make concessions, but they decided by and large to keep them in reserve, and throw them in at the last moment to close the deal. Critics who conducted a postmortem on the Common Market talks concluded that this was a mistaken policy, and that if the British Government had given more in the early stages, the country would have come off better in the end. On the other hand, it was felt in some quarters that however the British behaved, de Gaulle would have come out against them in the final stages.

As it was, many of the arguments at Brussels skirted the wider issues and got bogged down in petty details of trade in particular products. Though the delegates laid down the import duties on lead and linoleum, cricket bats and coconuts, they failed to agree on an overall trade policy. At the end of July 1962, in the closing stages of the year's work, the delegates held a marathon meeting centered not on British entry into the Common Market, but on the internal problem of finding a satisfactory agricultural policy for the Six. The Germans stubbornly contested the plan for a common price level for foodstuffs which they claimed would enrich the French at their expense. After two days and nights of continuous debate, the Germans capitulated in order to avoid an open break, and the meeting adjourned.

At this point the British agreed to remove their own agricultural subsidies if they were admitted to the Common Market, and in return the Six promised to study annual farm reviews and help farmers in areas which were hard hit by the common agricultural policy. When the delegates gathered up their piles of papers, packed their bags and departed to their various countries for the summer recess, they were exhausted—but not as yet without hope for the future.

While the British Conservatives worked toward cooperation with Europe, the Labour Party pulled in the reverse direction. Hugh Gaitskell, leader of the opposition, condemned Macmillan's "disastrous decision," and predicted a national catastrophe if Britain succeeded in joining the European club. This Labour campaign probably had a considerable effect on European thinking, for the leaders of the Six saw that if the Conservatives were defeated at the next election and the Labour Party took over the government, its independent policy would be likely to cause trouble in the Community.

On many fundamental issues the gap between Conservative and Labour Party policies has narrowed during recent years. Both parties favor wide schemes of social security: a national health service, old-age pensions, government education grants, unemployment benefits, and the provision of rent-controlled housing for those who need it. The Conservatives have accepted the necessity of nationalizing public transport, coal, gas and electricity.

But they still believe in a greater degree of free enterprise in industry than do their Labour opponents. They defend the private school system, whereby parents who are in a position to pay for their children's education are entitled to do so, while Labour left-wingers utterly condemn it. The Conservatives are in general more internationally minded, and they therefore found it easier to contemplate sacrificing a measure of British independence to Common Market control.

In the autumn of 1962 the Prime Ministers of the British dominions in Asia, Africa, North America and the Pacific gathered in London for the annual Commonwealth Conference. The meetings were stormy, but Macmillan did everything within his power to persuade the Commonwealth leaders not to stand in the way of British entry into the Common Market. He put forward two main lines of persuasion: first, an assurance that their relations with the European Economic Community would not be nearly as damaging as they feared; and second he tried to convince them that inside the Common Market, Britain would be in a strong financial position and able to help the Commonwealth, but outside it Britain would probably end up too weak to be of help to anyone. By eloquent appeal, Macmillan managed to stave off a motion of condemnation, and he brought the conference to an end without an open breach in Commonwealth relations.

14

THE BIG BREAKUP

In October 1962, shortly after the conclusion of the Commonwealth Conference in London, Edward Heath and the six Foreign Ministers with their attendant staffs returned to Brussels to continue the negotiations. By this time they had taken their places once more for the last act of the Common Market drama. By then most European governments had taken it almost for granted that the Six were so deeply involved, that British entry was really only a matter of time. Britain's EFTA partners had followed every move with close attention, and they were waiting for the Community countries to throw open their doors.

The American Government had, from the early days of the Marshall Plan, heartily supported European unity. They had done everything within their power to rebuild the wrecked economy and reestablish a sound political system. They hoped that a united Europe would lead to prosperity, and that the European nations would maintain good relations with the United States as partners in democratic government and friendly competitors in world trade. Leaders of successive administrations, both Democratic and Republican, had favored European solidarity, hoping that eventually the OEEC nations would not only be responsible for their own defense, but would also share the financial burden of promoting the welfare of the underdeveloped countries of the world.

Despite this pro-united-Europe policy, American leaders viewed the prospect of a greatly enlarged Common Market with some apprehension. From a political standpoint they thoroughly approved of British membership because it would add greater stability to the Community, and protect the small nations against French and German domination. But when they looked at the future from a practical standpoint, they were less happy because they saw trans-Atlantic trade difficulties ahead. It was apparent to economists that within the customs union formed by the Community countries, an increasing number of goods would be bought and sold without frontier duties; and that American goods going into Europe would be at a disadvantage because they would be subject to the rate of duty which the Six imposed on outside imports. Having contributed generously to European recovery when times were bad, the American Government was naturally anxious not to be left out in the cold now that they were good.

In the presidential election of 1960 a young Democrat, John F. Kennedy, had been chosen to succeed the elderly Republican, General Dwight D. Eisenhower, who had served two, four-year terms. John Kennedy was forty-three years old, the youngest President ever to be elected in the history of the United States, and he brought to the presidency immense energy, courage and idealism. He had need of all these qualities, for when he took over the leadership of the most powerful nation in the Western world he inherited a troubled state of affairs at home and a highly explosive situation abroad. Berlin was still disputed ground and a center of the Cold War in Europe; and Fidel Castro, ex-guerrilla fighter and sole ruler of the island republic of Cuba, had established a Communist stronghold in the Western hemisphere and was determined to destroy capitalist rule. In his inaugural speech Kennedy dedicated himself to the cause of world peace, but he did not underestimate Communist power, and he saw that the only way to treat with the Soviet bloc was from a position of strength. Therefore he wholeheartedly supported the Atlantic Alliance.

In October 1962, while the negotiators were assembling in Brussels, Khrushchev and Castro together tested Kennedy's resolution. American reconnaissance aircraft flying over Cuba discovered that an army of Soviet technicians had constructed launching sites on the island, and were in the process of installing medium and long-range ballistic missiles, all trained in the direction of the United States. On October 22, Kennedy broadcast to the American people, telling them of the Communist threat and announcing that he had ordered the United States Navy to blockade Cuba, to prevent any ship carrying offensive weapons from approaching the island. He warned Khrushchev that unless he agreed to remove the missiles, the United States would be forced to resort to armed force. For a week of dread and suspense the world waited, hovering on the brink of a third world war. Finally on October 29, faced by Kennedy's unrelenting ultimatum, and a strong denunciation by all the non-Communist countries in the United Nations, Khrushchev threw in his hand and consented to take out the missiles and dismantle the launching sites. Kennedy turned back to the pressing problems of Europe.

Kennedy sought advice from ardent "Europeans," among them Walter Hallstein, the first president of the European Economic Community Commission, who came to Washington for talks. Kennedy knew Jean Monnet personally and admired his capacity for clear thought and disinterested action. He shared Monnet's ideal of a united Europe, and applauded his aim of "a partnership of equals" between the United States and a strong European bloc. Working with able economic advisers Kennedy drafted a Trade Expansion Act by means of which he hoped to set tariffs at such a level that the United States would be able to expand its trade with the Common Market countries for the betterment of the Western world. It was a Grand Design for promoting trans-Atlantic trade, and to those who had taken part in its planning it ap-

Walter Hallstein confers with John F. Kennedy at the White House

peared to be a fine and feasible project. The Act was approved by the Senate and the House of Representatives in October 1962, while the Brussels negotiations were in full swing.

When President de Gaulle studied the Grand Design he condemned it violently, and declared that it was a trap to ensnare France and the other Common Market countries into subjection to the United States and Britain. He accused the British of trying to get into the Common Market simply to undermine his leadership and to become a go-between in American dealings with Europe. As the autumn wore on, de Gaulle's attitude hardened. Instead of giving consideration to the British case, he began to show outright displeasure at the idea of any form of partnership between Britain and the Six. The negotiators carried on with their work, though the outlook became increasingly bleak. Even then most people were not too worried; they felt that it made such good sense to team up with Britain that it was bound to work out all right in the end.

But suddenly relations between Macmillan and de Gaulle took a turn for the worse, and de Gaulle's smoldering exasperation at French nuclear backwardness came to an ugly head. Despite intensive research at vast expense, French progress in producing nuclear missiles and building bases and aircraft to launch them from was painfully slow. Members of opposition parties in the government were beginning to question whether the whole project, and the resulting drain on national resources, were worthwhile. Probably de Gaulle had hoped that once Britain was in the Common Market, Anglo-French cooperation would spread from industry to defense and that, with the help of British nuclear know-how, he would be able to form a French *force de frappe,* or nuclear striking force, independent of United States control.

In December 1962 a new development destroyed de Gaulle's hopes of a joint nuclear buildup with the British. For some years the United States and Britain had been discussing the production of a nuclear weapon known as Skybolt, and its place in the Atlantic defense program. Skybolt was a rocket-shaped missile designed to be launched from an aircraft as far as a thousand miles away from an enemy target. The general idea had been that it should be manufactured in the United States, and the warheads supplied to Britain in limited numbers, to be launched in case of need from Royal Air Force bombers—but only under United States orders. Little by little, American scientists were forced to admit that Skybolt was not a practical proposition. It proved to be terribly costly and difficult to perfect, and they decided to scrap it and concentrate instead on Polaris, a nuclear weapon designed for launching from special submarines.

After considerable consultation with his Chiefs-of-Staff, Kennedy summoned Macmillan to a meeting on the Caribbean island of Nassau to break the news of the Skybolt failure and plan a joint strategy for Polaris. He did not at this point extend the invitation to de Gaulle, for he distrusted French nationalistic nuclear aims. The American President offered the British Prime Minister Polaris missiles for a fleet of submarines to be placed under NATO command, and operated by a crew drawn from a number of different NATO nations. Macmillan was disturbed by the failure of Skybolt, but he accepted the offer, and Kennedy immediately offered the new missile to de Gaulle on precisely the same terms.

By Christmastime, the leaders of the member countries of the Atlantic Alliance were at cross purposes. Kennedy spoke confidently of growing unity of purpose, policy and power; while de Gaulle retired to Colombey for the festive season to brood on the eclipse of French power, and to decide on his future strategy. He was impelled by a passionate desire for French supremacy, and also evidently by extreme personal ambition. Eventually he turned down the Polaris offer and pressed on with French nuclear development.

In de Gaulle's New Year's message to the nation, it became perfectly clear that he had made up his mind to veto British entry into the European Economic Community. At a press conference on January 14, he announced that Britain was not sufficiently "European" to be an acceptable candidate for membership; and that the British were not yet "ready" to become loyal partners in Community plans and purposes. He referred to Britain as a satellite of the United States and a disrupting influence in European unity. With a single blow he destroyed the solidarity of the Common Market and demolished the Grand Design. Many of his ministers protested; they said that every other member of the Six was in favor of Britain's entry, and that France would be isolated. Edward Heath rushed to Paris to seek reassurance from Couve de Murville, but the Foreign Minister was not in a position to give a satisfactory answer.

In Brussels the meetings continued in an atmosphere fraught with uncertainty and foreboding. Britain made some further concessions on outstanding farm issues which, France willing, would have gone a long way toward meeting Common Market demands. But, in the circumstances, they were received with glum faces and scant enthusiasm, yet almost everyone felt that somehow, somewhere, there must be a solution, and a Common Market conjurer would bring something good out of a hat.

On January 29, Couve de Murville, looking tired and very tense, arrived in Brussels to pronounce the final verdict of his government. He told the crowded gathering of official negotiators and members of the world press that France would exercise the right of veto to block British entry. The French decision was greeted by an outburst of angry protests, and almost universal expressions of despondency and shame. The Foreign Ministers spoke in turn, each one openly condemning the French action. Professor Hallstein, President of the Common Market Commission which had played a major part in the negotiations, spoke of the outcome with deep regret. Finally, Edward Heath soberly acknowledged defeat, and the negotiations came to an end.

In the aftermath of Brussels, de Gaulle remained outwardly unmoved. A week before the final climax,

The British delegation after the breakdown of negotiations with the Common Market

conscious that he was losing support all over Europe, he had tightened the bonds of Franco-German friendship by signing a Treaty of Cooperation with Konrad Adenauer. It was one of Adenauer's last official acts in keeping with his whole concept of peace in Europe. The following summer, at the age of eighty-seven, he resigned his post as Chancellor, though he remained a member of the

Bundestag until his death four years later. Adenauer was succeeded by Ludwig Erhard, also a Christian Democrat, who had served very efficiently as Minister of Economics and proved himself both able and popular in Western Europe. Throughout his public life Erhard had been a liberal thinker, strongly in favor of free trade between nations. He came to office at a time of crisis in Common Market affairs, and although he maintained good relations with France, he considered it even more important to strengthen trade links with the United States than to work closely with de Gaulle.

After Britain's dismissal, the governments of Northern Ireland, Denmark and Norway—which had already applied for membership in the Common Market—did not pursue the matter any further.

The French veto shook the Common Market to its foundations. The leaders of the Community countries, especially those in Italy and the Benelux states, lost faith in de Gaulle and looked for other leadership. Although the economic program continued according to plan, something went out of the original spirit of the Treaty of Rome.

But the Common Market was a new venture, and the fact that it survived the Brussels crisis at all proved that it had sufficient strength to withstand reverses. In six years it had built up a backbone of European prosperity, and the people of the Community countries were better off than they had ever been before.

On November 22, 1963 John Kennedy was murdered by a fanatical gunman in Dallas. The world mourned the tragedy, but his work went on. The Grand Design gave way to a series of widespread trade negotiations known to the associated governments as the "Kennedy Round." For four arduous years forty-nine countries, with the Six working together as a single unit, bargained on a reduction of their trade tariffs. It is remarkable that in 1967 they agreed on a schedule which covered four-fifths of the trade of the whole world, and succeeded in reducing tariffs by over a third.

By this time political power had changed hands in Britain. The Labour Party won the general election in October 1964, and Harold Wilson became Prime Minister and George Brown Foreign Minister. They inherited the traditional fear of the British Labour Party of loosing national independence through European entanglements. But industrial stagnation at home, and mounting production among the Six, finally drew them toward the Common Market.

Early in 1967 Wilson and Brown set out on a tour of the Common Market capitals, to sound out opinion on a new British approach. In general the reaction was friendly, and on May 2, the Prime Minister announced in the House of Commons that his government had decided to apply once more for admission.

The three Communities had recently merged their separate Councils and Commissions into two central bodies, both of which put the British application, with those of Ireland, Denmark and Norway, on the agenda for immediate discussion.

But by the end of the year the Council of Ministers and the Commission had reached a deadlock. Once more President de Gaulle blocked British entry. He predicted that new negotiations would be the death knell of the Common Market, and there was nothing the other five could do to reverse his judgment. The British Government refused to withdraw its application, so it remains on the agenda, but it seemed that while the General lived, or at least remained in control, there was little hope of getting in. In 1967 de Gaulle was seventy-six and old men seldom change their minds on things that really matter.

However, in June 1969 General de Gaulle proclaimed a referendum throughout France. The French people had to cast a single vote, simply "Yes" or "No," on two very different questions. The first was the reform of the Constitution, the second the question of giving more authority to regional government. The referendum turned out to be a vote of confidence for the aged general, because he announced that if the "Noes" outnumbered the "Yeses" he would resign instantly. Slogans on the walls, buildings, shop windows, sidewalks and road surfaces in the cities, towns and villages throughout France reflected public opinion; and when the votes were counted de Gaulle was defeated. He had grown overconfident of his position, and had lost touch with popular feeling. The people were tired of proclamations of grandeur, and were seeking normal leadership. He retired according to his promise, but many Frenchmen who had voted against him were saddened by the manner of his going. In many ways de Gaulle was a great man, and he left without a single public tribute. It was the end of an era.

De Gaulle was succeeded as President by Georges Pompidou, a Gaullist who had served under him, but evidently differed from his policy on some important issues. Pompidou chose as his Premier, Jacques Chaban-Delmas and as his Foreign Minister, Maurice Schumann, men noted for their liberal views. The widening of the Common Market once more became a matter of the moment. Britain remained the forerunner of the candidate nations, and it seemed that after de Gaulle's departure, British entry depended more on economic negotiation and mutual concession than on political prejudice.

In the autumn of 1969 there was a general election in West Germany and for the first time since the foundation of the Federal Republic, the Christian Democrats failed to win a working majority. The Social Democrats, a left-wing party, formed a coalition with a small Free Democrat group and Willy Brandt, former mayor of the Western sector of Berlin, became Chancellor.

The two main differences in policy between Konrad Adenauer's Christian Democrats and Willy Brandt's Social Democrats lie first in their attitude to the Communist-ruled German Democratic Republic, and second to the admission of Britain and the other candidate countries to the Common Market. Soon after his election to the Chancellorship, Brandt acknowledged the existence of a republic in East Germany as a political fact, whereas Adenauer had always spoken of the ultimate reunification of the whole of Germany as a definite political aim. Brandt refers to the people of East Germany as "neighbors" who have "relations of a special nature with the people of the Federal Republic." He has also spoken out strongly in favor of holding talks with Britain to negotiate the broadening of the Common Market and the extension of European unity.

15

THE COMMON MARKET TODAY

A BRIEF SUMMARY of Common Market industrial progress since the Treaty of Rome came into effect in 1958 makes impressive reading. In economic affairs, the Six have advanced side by side according to the plans of the Spaak committee, confirmed by the Treaty of Rome. In 1962 Greece, and in 1964 Turkey, became associated members with a view to full membership in the future. In 1968 the Six reached two very important stages on the road to total economic integration. On July 1, eighteen months ahead of the appointed time, they completed their customs union, and removed the remaining duties and tariff restrictions on trade in industrial goods of every kind passing from one Community country to another. A few months later the Six granted full freedom of movement to all their workers, so that with a "European" labor card a skilled technician, steel worker, baker, tailor or builder can apply for a job wherever he sees the best opportunities, and an employer can take him on without having to go through all the red tape of obtaining government permission.

It is disappointing to the men who are working to fulfill the terms of the Treaties that, although they have opened the way for the free transfer of money from one Community country to another, they have not been able to carry it out in practice. Because of internal financial conditions governments have been compelled to revalue their currencies. In order to protect their reserve funds they have had to limit the amount of money that public companies or private individuals take out of their own countries; and though these restrictions have hampered the management of Common Market finance, they are essential to the economic survival of the countries concerned.

Nevertheless, through the installation of new equipment, the introduction of modern working methods, and the gradual lowering of frontier restrictions, the rate of production and the volume of trade within the Community has exceeded the most optimistic expectations. In the first nine years of Common Market existence, the overall industrial output of the Community increased by sixty-seven percent. This figure compares with the United States rise in production of seventy-two percent during the same period, and more than doubles the British rise of thirty-three percent.

People in the Community countries are better housed and fed than they were in 1958, and there is now very little unemployment. Coordinated government schemes provide wider education and greater social security than they did ten years ago. In the Western world people are very apt to regard the possession of a car as a symbol of success. By this standard the people of the Common Market countries are doing well, for in 1958 only one in every ten owned a car, while today the number of car owners has risen to one in every six. More motor vehicles of various kinds roll off the Common Market assembly lines than in any other industrial bloc in the world, except the United States.

Owing to their industrial success the Six have started to close the gap between United States affluence and Western European poverty. When the nations assembled for the talks on the Kennedy Round, the Common Market delegates came prepared to negotiate on equal terms, not—as formerly—to seek American bounty.

The customs union was a tremendous step forward, for it simplified and speeded up the already flourishing trade between the Six. Since it came into force, factories in Milan, Dusseldorf or Luxembourg can turn out goods and sell them in Paris, Brussels or Amsterdam just as easily as manufacturers in Pittsburgh or Detroit can sell their goods in New York.

This customs union does not mean that similar makes and categories of goods are sold for the same prices throughout the Community. Wages vary from one country to the next, and as it costs more to make an electric light bulb in Germany than in Italy, and more to make a three-wave transistor radio in France than in

Germany, their higher production costs are reflected by higher selling prices in the shops.

It is part of Common Market policy to accept a variation in industrial prices according to the quality of a particular article and its cost of production. In this way there is reasonable competition between enterprising firms, and an incentive to produce high-standard goods. As things stand at present, Common Market shoppers can look over the wide range of merchandise without the feeling that they are paying the penalty of import duty if they happen to select a foreign-made article.

It would be dishonest to pretend that this satisfactory industrial progress is entirely due to the foresighted provisions of the Treaty of Rome. The inhabitants of the Six are mainly industrious people with a tradition of hard work behind them, and in this era of technical achievement, they would undoubtedly have increased their output in the ordinary course of events. But as they have succeeded in doubling the British increase in rate of production, it appears that the pooling of skills and resources, and working to a plan prepared by men of high intelligence and "European" ideals, pays a handsome dividend.

So far the principles of the founding Treaties of the Community have been tested mainly in the economic affairs of the Six. The results can be counted by politicians and bankers, merchants and manufacturers in francs, marks, lire and florins. There is no doubt that the experi-

A shop in the European Economic Community

ment in European integration has proved well worthwhile. The strands of solidarity have been severely strained by conflicting opinions, but they have always held. At times of acute crisis, when the interests of the member countries clashed, they have always managed to find a compromise. The importance of preserving the Common Market as a whole has tipped the balance against national interest, and the people have developed a sense of security and mutual pride in belonging to a Community of nations.

Common Market policy has worked out better in industry than in agriculture. Industrial conditions can, to a large extent, be brought into line and production is predictable. But farming conditions are variable, and production depends on the soil and the weather and they cannot be measured with a slide rule or accurately assessed with a computer.

There are, however, considerable successes to record. Agricultural wages have risen, living conditions have improved, and mechanization is advancing steadily, but the problem of the food surpluses remains and common pricing has turned out to be unworkable.

In 1969, after the French and German revaluations, the financial and agricultural experts of the European Economic Community Commission did some intensive rethinking. As a result, they agreed to exempt France and Germany from the common pricing rules, and this in itself was a considerable relaxation of policy. But it does not mean that the whole agricultural system has broken down. Payments into and out of the common fund pass from country to country and are used for the common good. They link agricultural projects, help needy farmers, and support government retraining schemes for farmers who want to leave the land and find new jobs.

Now that the Commission has faced up to the economic facts of farm life, future discussions should be more constructive, decisions less rigid and the possibilities of agreement greater. It should be easier to sort out the complications of Common Market farming and find a working compromise. Since Germany has been permitted by the Commission to adopt a system of farm subsidies very similar to that which the British Government has been operating since the end of the Second World War, many of the former arguments against the entry of Britain, Ireland, Denmark and Norway into the Common Market no longer hold good.

All in all 1969 was a most eventful year. It started badly with a general sense of frustration and depression after the failure of the Brussels negotiations and the consequent conflict of opinion among the Six. When General de Gaulle was succeeded by President Pompidou, and Chancellor Erhard by Willy Brandt, the tension relaxed. The new heads of states not only saw eye to eye with each other, but they also drew together the leaders of the other Common Market countries. Moreover they were anxious to build up a better relationship with the United States and Britain. On December 1 and 2, the heads of government of the Six Community countries, with their Foreign Ministers, held a Summit Meeting at The Hague to discuss current problems. The question of reopening negotiations on the question of British entry stood high on the agenda. President Pompidou was wary in his preliminary speech, and he insisted that the Community should settle its agricultural difficulties before considering the admission of new members. But when the meeting opened Willy Brandt threw his full weight behind Britain's bid for membership. He said: "Our choice is between a courageous step forward and a dangerous crisis." He stressed the advantages of working with Britain, for it was a two way gain—Britain needed a firm foothold in Europe and the Common Market needed British political, technical and industrial collaboration.

The final communique issued at the end of the Summit Meeting gave new hope for the future of European unity and new life to the Community. It was agreed that negotiations for British entry should begin by mid-summer 1970, and it was assumed that the financial arrangements for Common Market agriculture would have been completed long beforehand. The conference also reached a tentative agreement on the revision of the whole system of Common Market finance by January 1971. Instead of being dependent on contributions from the various governments for money to cover current expenses, these funds would be collected from the duties levied on industrial and agricultural goods imported from countries outside the Six. This would mean that the Common Market would be financially independent, paying its own way through its actual earnings. There was also considerable discussion on extending the budgetary powers of the European Parliament and giving it the final word in how Common Market money should be used. In addition, the communique expressed a determination to strengthen the political links of the Community countries. The Six agreed to extend their technical cooperation and nuclear research. It seems that a period of Common Market conflict and uncertainty has ended and a period of positive action has begun. The Hague Meeting closed in a spirit of optimism and faith in the future of Europe; and the year 1969 ended much more happily than it had begun.

It is probably too early to predict how soon and to what extent political union will develop from the present state of economic partnership. Even the most passionate pioneers of European unity realized that the United States of Europe could only be approached by gradual integration and achieved by growing goodwill. Men like Jean Monnet, Paul-Henri Spaak, Konrad Adenauer and Alcide de Gasperi laid the foundations and built the framework of European unity. Now it remains for the leaders of the younger generation to complete the structure. They will have to decide what kind of Europe they want to live in, and they will need to be convinced that nationalism leads to war and that international cooperation offers the best hope of keeping the world at peace.

BIBLIOGRAPHY

Balfour, Michael. *West Germany*. New York: Frederick A. Praeger, Inc., 1967.

Beloff, Nora. *The General Says No*. Baltimore: Penguin Books, Inc., 1963.

Broad, Roger and Jarrett, Robert. *Community Europe*. New York: Humanities Press, Inc., 1967.

Calmann, John. *Western Europe: A Handbook*. New York: Frederick A. Praeger, Inc., 1967.

Camps, Miriam. *What Kind of Europe?* Royal Institute of International Affairs. New York: Oxford University Press, 1965.

The Common Market and the Common Man. European Communities Press and Information, July, 1969.

Deniau, Jean F. *The Common Market*. New York: Fernhill House, Ltd., 1967.

Ellis, Harry B. *The Common Market*. New York: World Publishing Co., 1965.

Galante, Pierre. *The General*. New York: Random House, 1969.

The Parliament of the European Communities. Vol. XXX, No. 478. Political and Economic Planning, London, 1964.

Pinder, John and Pryce, Roy. *Europe After De Gaulle*. Baltimore: Penguin Books, 1969.

Sampson, Anthony. *The New Europeans.* London: Hodder and Stoughton, 1968.

Schlesinger, Arthur M., Jr. *A Thousand Days: John F. Kennedy in the White House.* Boston: Houghton Mifflin Co., 1965.

Treaty Establishing the EEC (Rome Treaty). London: Her Majesty's Stationery Office, 1958.

Werth, Alexander. *De Gaulle.* Baltimore: Penguin Books, Inc., 1967.

Publications of the European Community Information Service. London.

INDEX

C

UI
L

A

A